OXFORD Classic Playscripts

Lady Macbeth

CITY OF
LEARNING
CENTRE
SUNDERLAND COLLEGE

David Calcutt

OXFORD
UNIVERSITY PRESS

D1101820

Great Clarendon Street, Oxford OX2 6DP

Oxford University Press is a department of the University of Oxford.
It furthers the University's objective of excellence in research,
scholarship, and education by publishing worldwide in

Oxford   New York

Auckland   Cape Town   Dar es Salaam   Hong Kong   Karachi
Kuala Lumpur   Madrid   Melbourne   Mexico City   Nairobi
New Delhi   Shanghai   Taipei   Toronto

With offices in

Argentina   Austria   Brazil   Chile   Czech Republic   France   Greece
Guatemala   Hungary   Italy   Japan   Poland   Portugal   Singapore
South Korea   Switzerland   Thailand   Turkey   Ukraine   Vietnam

Oxford is a registered trade mark of Oxford University Press
in the UK and in certain other countries

British Library Cataloguing in Publication Data

Data available

ISBN-13: 978 0 19 832083 8

ISBN-10: 0 19 832083 3

10 9 8 7 6 5 4 3 2 1

Compiled by Q2A Creative.

Printed by Creative Print and Design Wales, Ebbw Vale.

Acknowledgements

Artwork is by Martin Cottam.

Cover image by Photodisc.

Contents

General Introduction

With a fresh, modern look, this classroom-friendly series boasts an exciting range of authors – from Pratchett to Chaucer – whose works have been expertly adapted by such well-known and popular writers as Philip Pullman and David Calcutt. We have also divided the titles available (see page X) into subcategories – OXFORD *Classic Playscripts* and OXFORD *Modern Playscripts* – to make it even easier for you to think about titles – and periods – you wish to study.

Many teachers use OXFORD *Playscripts* to study the format, style, and structure of playscripts with their students; for speaking and listening assignments; to initiate discussion of relevant issues in class; to meet the Drama objectives of the Framework; as an introduction to the novel of the same title; and to introduce the less able or willing to pre-1914 literature.

At the back of each OXFORD *Playscript*, you will find a brand new Activity section, which not only addresses the points above, but also features close text analysis, and activities that provide support for underachieving readers and act as a springboard for personal writing. Furthermore, the new Activity sections now match precisely the Framework Objectives for Teaching English at Key Stage 3; a chart mapping the Objectives – and the activities that cover them – can be found at the beginning of each Activity section.

Many schools will simply read through the play in class with no staging at all, and the Activity sections have been written with this in mind, with individual activities ranging from debates and designing campaign posters to writing extra scenes or converting parts of the original novels into playscript form.

For those of you, however, who do wish to take to the stage, each OXFORD *Playscript* also features 'A Note on Staging' – a section dedicated to suggesting ways of staging the play, as well as examining the props and sets you may wish to use.

Above all, we hope you will enjoy using OXFORD *Playscripts*, be it on the stage or in the classroom.

What the Playwright Says

The Idea

My original idea was to write a play which told the story of *Macbeth* from the points of view of several characters from Shakespeare's play. So, we would have Banquo's version of events, Macduff's, Donalbain's, the Porter's, and so on. The plan was to divide the story up into separate episodes, and to have each episode narrated by a different character. One of these episodes would be narrated by Lady Macbeth.

The Research

Next, I decided to do some research into the historical facts behind Shakespeare's portrayal of his characters in order to give them a context outside of *Macbeth*. It so happened that the character I started with was Lady Macbeth, and I became so absorbed in her story that she began to take over the whole play. I discovered, for instance, that she was, in fact, a Pictish princess.

  The Picts were the original inhabitants of the land we now call Scotland. The Scots, on the other hand, were an Irish tribe who came across and gradually took over the country from the Picts, eventually outlawing their culture. Lady Macbeth's father was one of the last Pictish kings. I also found out that, before she married Macbeth, Lady Macbeth was married to another Scottish lord, and had a child by him.

The New Idea

All this research began to give me an idea of Lady Macbeth's character which was, in many ways, quite different to the one presented to us by Shakespeare. The fact of her Pictish inheritance, and that she had to survive in a world that was hostile to her, gave a real dramatic tension to her character. So, I abandoned my original idea, and went instead with the idea of writing a play about Lady Macbeth. I still think the first idea's a good one, though, and may well use it in some future play.

More Research

I did most of my research using the Internet. For example, I found large sections of Holinshead's *Chronicles* there, the book that Shakespeare used as his source material. Examining the *Chronicles*, I was surprised to find how much Shakespeare himself had actually changed from the original content. The wife who urges her husband to murder the king, for instance, was in fact taken from another story, and doesn't belong to Lady Macbeth and Macbeth at all. I also found a surprising amount of detailed information about the historical Lady Macbeth, and about the Picts in general. Of course, all this information can also be found in books, but it would have made the whole research process a lot longer.

When I'm doing research, I make notes of everything I think will be of use in the play, and then later type these notes up for use in the writing process. Sometimes, something I've made notes on will suggest an entire scene, or give me a way of gaining insight into a character. Similarly, when I'm writing, I usually scribble some lines of dialogue, or a piece of narrative, quite roughly, into a notebook, and then work from those when I type up the scene on my PC. Often, too, I'll be working one scene, when I have an idea for another scene, or episode, for much later in the play, and it's important that I write that down into my notebook right away, so that I don't forget it!

The Poetic Form

As you'll know, if you've studied any of his plays, Shakespeare makes good use of iambic pentameter* in his writing. This was something I wanted to use in my play, too, but I was also keen to use prose, and other forms of verse. I believe that a writer should use whatever form of language seems appropriate for the particular scene or episode that's being written.

The beauty about writing in iambic pentameter is that it has a fairly strict form and pattern and, once you get this pattern into your head, you can shape what you want to write to fit it. Sometimes, how you write is dictated to you by the pattern itself, and you find yourself writing something you may never have thought of if you hadn't had that pattern! In a sense it's quite liberating, and the language can sometimes flow quite easily when you're writing in that way. Too much choice, too much freedom, can have the effect of blocking the flow of writing, whereas the tighter boundaries of poetic form can release it – it's strange!

The Next Steps

Once the first draft of a script has been typed up, then the really hard work begins – that's the writing and re-writing, cutting, editing – knocking the whole thing into shape. It's the hardest bit, but it is the most important. In the same way that first thoughts aren't always the best, and can be improved by further and deeper reflection, so the first thing you write can often be improved by looking and working at it several times over. This is where an editor can be more than helpful. A good editor will act as your objective eye, be able to stand a little further back from the piece, see more clearly where improvements can be made, things deleted or added so that, between you, you can come up with a script that tells the story in the most dramatic and effective way possible. And I hope this one does that!

David Calcutt

★ The term *iambic pentameter* describes the poetic form where each line has ten beats (or syllables) and where those beats are divided into pairs, known as *iambic feet*. Each iambic foot contains one stressed and one unstressed syllable.

A Note on Staging

Costumes and Personal Props

Items you may need include:

the **Girl**: flowers (to put in her hair).

the **Goodwife**: a (cooking) pot.

the **Crone**: a wooden staff.

Gruach/Lady Macbeth: 3 small dolls; a mask of Death; a dagger; a bracelet; rings; a necklace; a gold crown; a cloak 'lined with ermine'.

Beoedhe's Ghost: a staff; rags (for clothing); a bloody rag (for his eyes).

Magg: a dagger; a small bottle (of potion).

Grimm: a bag containing miscellaneous pieces of loot.

Thorfinn/Macbeth: a sword; a crown; a bag of coins.

Finnleach: a helmet; a mask; a sword; a golden chain; a belt with a silver buckle, studded with gems; a gold ring.

MacRory: a helmet; a mask; a sword.

Lady Macduff: two small bags of coins.

Soldiers 1–8: masks; armour; heavy swords; shields.

Nurse: a doll (as Gruach's child); 'a shawl of woven wool, red and green' and 'a blanket of fleece' (in which to wrap her child).

The Stage

The set for the entire play consists of three large standing stones, worn and ancient. One stands centre stage, the other two on either side of it; together, they form a semi-circle in which the play will be performed.

All three stones are inscribed with figures and symbols: some abstract geometric patterns, such as circles and spirals; others more figurative and representational – sun, moon, animal and human characters.

There is a small pool of water within the stones.

The Real Macbeth, Shakespeare's Macbeth and Lady Macbeth

The Real Macbeth

Macbeth is more than just a character in a play. A Scottish nobleman, he was born in around 1005, into a powerful family that ruled the Scottish lands of Moray and Ross. It was a violent time and battles for power were common, even within families and clans. In fact, Macbeth's own father was murdered by his cousins.

The historical Macbeth was descended from Malcolm II of Scotland (his grandfather), so he was in a strong position to become king himself. He married the granddaughter of a High King of Scotland, Gruach, and moved upwards through the ranks to become Mormaer ('great steward') of Moray, a position of almost royal authority.

It is said that, at this time, the rule of Duncan – king of the part of Scotland that is now Strathclyde – was unpopular. As a grandson of Malcolm II, Macbeth may also have resented Duncan's position – especially as he was expected to become King of Scotland himself. Whatever his motives, Macbeth seized Duncan's throne by force and was elected High King of Scotland in around 1040.

Shakespeare's Macbeth

In his famous play, Shakespeare takes the historical facts about Macbeth and uses them to create a play about ambition, power, greed and murder.

At the beginning of the play, Duncan is King of Scotland and Macbeth one of his loyal thanes. As he is leaving a battlefield, Macbeth and his friend, Banquo, meet three Witches, who tell Macbeth that he will be promoted before becoming king himself. They also tell Banquo that, although he will never be king like Macbeth, his sons will sit on the throne for years to come.

Driven by a desire for absolute power, Macbeth – encouraged by Lady Macbeth, his wife – murders Duncan in his sleep. After Duncan's death, Macbeth is indeed crowned king, but he is unable to relax: Banquo's sons are destined to succeed him to the throne, and Duncan's sons are busy raising an army to overthrow him, together with another nobleman, Macduff. In fits of greedy fear, Macbeth arranges the murders of Banquo and his son, and of Macduff's entire family.

By this time, however, both Macbeth and his wife are racked with guilt: Macbeth hallucinates, and Lady Macbeth has started walking in her sleep and is showing signs of insanity. As the army led by Macduff and the dead king's sons approaches Macbeth's castle, Lady Macbeth kills herself. Not long afterwards, Macbeth is killed in battle by Macduff.

Lady Macbeth

In *Lady Macbeth*, David Calcutt uses a combination of historical fact and Shakespeare's *Macbeth* as the basis for a new play: it is the story of Gruach, a Pictish princess (see 'The Real Macbeth' above).

A new religion is sweeping Scotland and wiping out the native Picts: Christianity. The Pictish king, Beoedhe, has been captured by MacRory, the Christian heir to the Scottish throne, and is banished from the land. MacRory then takes Beoedhe's daughter, Gruach, as his wife. The plot that then unfolds has Gruach – later Lady Macbeth – at its centre: we follow her from girlhood, to womanhood, to motherhood, and we watch as she bargains with the Wyrd Sisters and grapples with her fate.

With the focus here on Lady Macbeth, the story begins before Shakespeare's play does – before the Macbeths are married – and ends with Gruach's despair and death. It is a story that suggests possible motives behind the Macbeths' ambition, in doing so moving away from Shakespeare's Macbeth and taking us back towards the historical characters of 1040.

Characters

the **Girl**
the **Goodwife**   the **Wyrd Sisters**
the **Crone**

Gruach, later **Lady Macbeth**   a Pictish princess, later Lady Macbeth and
                                       Queen of Scotland
Beoedhe (and **Beoedhe's Ghost**) **Gruach**'s father, a Pictish king
Gruach's child★   **Gruach**'s son; his father is (**Thorfinn**) **Macbeth**

Magg   a couple 'living on [their] wits', frequently on
Grimm   the wrong side of the law

Thorfinn, later **Macbeth**   a Scottish nobleman, later **Macbeth** and King
                                       of Scotland
Finnleach   **Thorfinn**'s father

Malcolm   King of Scotland
Duncan   **Malcolm**'s nephew
MacRory Gillacomgain   **Malcolm**'s appointed heir

Lady Macduff   a noblewoman; her husband, Macduff, the
                                       Thane★★ of Fife, poses a threat to **Macbeth**'s
                                       throne

Soldier 1
Soldier 2
Soldier 3
Soldier 4   soldiers in **MacRory**'s army
Soldier 5
Soldier 6
Soldier 7
Soldier 8

★   *As Gruach's child is only a baby in this play, a doll is best used for the part.*
★★ *thane – a man ranking above an ordinary freeman and below a noble in Anglo Saxon*
    England, especially one who gave military service in exchange for land

a **Captain**
Northman 1
Northman 2
Northman 3

a **Nurse**
a **Messenger**
a **Servant**

soldiers in **Duncan**'s army

Gruach's son's wet nurse

Scene 1

*Enter **Gruach**. She crosses to a pool near three large standing stones and kneels before it.*

Gruach　There are three.

She takes out a small doll and places it on the floor beside her.

First, the girl.

*Enter the **Girl**, from behind one of the standing stones.*

Girl　Carefree, innocent. She skips, she sings, she wears flowers in her hair. Pulls the wings off flies. Blows up frogs with a straw till they burst. Pop!

Gruach　And all the time she laughs, for the whole world's her playground.

*The **Girl** takes up position in front of her stone. **Gruach** takes out a second doll and sets it down.*

Next, the goodwife.

*Enter the **Goodwife** from behind another of the standing stones.*

Goodwife　Red-faced and cheery, smells of washing and apples. She can cure any ailment with her herbs and oils. Carries her pot wherever she goes, and she'll cook you a stew to put meat on your bones.

Gruach	But who's to say what's in it, and who can tell whose flesh you eat?
	*The **Goodwife** takes up position in front of her stone. **Gruach** takes out a third doll and sets it down.*
	And last, the crone.
	*Enter the **Crone** from behind the third standing stone. She carries a wooden staff.*
Crone	Black holes for eyes, but she sees deep. Sees the things that crawl in the cellar of your soul. Only one tooth in her head, but it's sharp as a blade. Sharp as the moon's edge and it bites to the bone.
Gruach	She'll wind your corpse and weep over your grave … and raise you up from it and set you dancing.
Girl	Three stones.
Goodwife	Three women.
Crone	Us. Wyrd sisters.
Sisters	We weave the webs That bind men fast, From breath to death From first to last. From joy to pain, From grave to birth, We set men walking On the earth, And shape their fates With tales and songs, And tell their lives With crooked tongues.
Girl	And it's her tale we're telling…
Goodwife	Her life's web we're weaving…
Crone	Her death-shroud we're winding…
Girl	This woman, who called us up out of the stones…
Goodwife	Ancient stones, rooted in earth…

Crone	From the dark of the earth she called us up…
Girl	From the dark of the blood that runs in her veins…
Goodwife	The blood of those who first walked this land…
Crone	Who named its hills and raised these stones…
Sisters	And all that remains are dust and bones.
Girl	Speak her name.
Goodwife	Fix her here.
Crone	As she's fixed us. Speak her name.
Girl	Gruach.
Goodwife	Gruach.
Crone	Gruach.
Gruach	*[Turning]* Who's there? Who speaks my name? Who is it?
Girl	She looks, but sees no one…
Goodwife	Only these stones, standing on the hillside.
Crone	She listens, but hears nothing…
Girl	Only the cold voice of the wind…
Goodwife	That moans on the hillside…
Crone	That whispers through the grasses.
Girl	Gruach.
Goodwife	Gruach.
Crone	Gruach.
Gruach	*[Turning back to the pool]* No one. There's no one there.
	*Gruach carries out the actions as now described by the **Wyrd Sisters**.*
Girl	Now she kneels by the pool…
Goodwife	Bends over it, cups her hands…
Crone	Dips her cupped hands into the water…
Girl	Raises them to her mouth…
Goodwife	Sucks up the cold water out of her cupped hands…

Crone	Splashes the rest of it over her face…
Sisters	And now she's ready, and speaks her prayer.
Gruach	New moon, old moon, Dark and bright; Waxing, waning, Silver bright. Show to me The face of he That my own true love shall be.
Girl	This is what she wants…
Goodwife	The reason she's called us…
Crone	To see the face of her own dear love.
Girl	And she'll see it.
Goodwife	We'll show her.
Crone	We'll grant this woman her heart's desire.
Girl	But the face that she sees will be bloody…
Goodwife	And the eyes in that face will be filled with death.
Crone	A soldier's face, a killer's face.
Girl	A face cased in armour.
Goodwife	A face in a mask.
Crone	And the mask that it wears is the mask of war.

Gruach and the *Wyrd Sisters* remain onstage for the next scene.

Scene 2

*Enter the **Soldiers**, one by one, on their lines. All are masked, armoured, and carry heavy swords and shields. They take up positions around the stage, facing each other. Their voices are taunting, hate-filled.*

Soldier 1	*[Entering]* Ancient grudges.
Soldier 2	*[Entering]* Rival factions.
Soldier 3	*[Entering]* Clan warfare.
Soldier 4	*[Entering]* Tribal strife.
Soldier 5	*[Entering]* An insult given.
Soldier 6	*[Entering]* A vow broken.
Soldier 7	*[Entering]* A curse from heaven.
Soldier 8	*[Entering]* A life taken.
Soldier 1	Blood's been spilled.
Soldier 2	Blood's been shed.
Soldier 3	A cousin killed.
Soldier 4	A brother dead.
Soldier 5	Battle-shout.
Soldier 6	War-cry.
Soldier 7	Swords clash.
Soldier 8	Men die.

*The **Soldiers** freeze, as if ready for battle.*

Girl	And who knows how it started?
Goodwife	Who remembers, and who cares?
Crone	The cause is not their concern…
Girl	Only that the argument is settled.
Goodwife	And this is how the argument is always settled.

Crone	With blood.
Soldiers	*[Chanting softly throughout the **Wyrd Sisters'** next speech]* Blood, blood, blood, etc. …
Sisters	The earth needs blood To make it grow, The hills to rise, The streams to flow; The heather's bloom, The oak tree's root, The hawthorn leaf, Each bud and shoot. Bones in the ground, A corpse in the ditch, Makes the land Both fat and rich. And so this law Holds firm and good, Then men must die And spill their blood.

*Continuing to chant, the **Soldiers** now begin to beat their swords against their shields. Enter **Finnleach** and **MacRory**, both helmeted and masked.*

MacRory	Turn, hell-hound! Stay! Now, wilt thou fight with me?
Finnleach	I shall, while there's still armour on my back.
MacRory	Unfix thy sword, and screw thy courage fast.
Finnleach	The blade is drawn, and burns for thy hot blood.
MacRory	Speak no more words!
Finnleach	My sword shall speak for me!
MacRory	Fight on!
Finnleach	Until death claims us!
MacRory	Thee or me!

*They fight. **MacRory** gets the upper hand.*

MacRory	I have thee at the stake.

Finnleach	But like a bear I'll bite.
	*They fight on. Now **Finnleach** gets the upper hand.*
Finnleach	Cry 'Hold!' and I'll give thee thy life.
MacRory	My life's mine own, and I'll cry 'Death!' to thee.
	They fight on once more, then come to a deadlock.
MacRory	Our horns are locked. Will you give ground?
Finnleach	Not I.
MacRory	Nor I. Yet one must live.
Finnleach	And one must die.
	*The **Crone** stamps the ground with her staff. The **Soldiers** fall silent. **MacRory** and **Finnleach** freeze.*
Girl	Which one?
Goodwife	Who shall it be?
Crone	I'll choose.
	*She crosses to **MacRory** and **Finnleach**, and touches **MacRory** with her staff.*
	This man's cold-hearted, merciless, cruel. He dreams of power, his fist gripped tight on the land.
	*She moves to **Finnleach** and touches him with her staff.*
	This man's honest, merciful, fair. A courageous spirit, a good heart. He loves the land like a child loves its mother.
	*She considers a moment, then touches **Finnleach** again.*
	This one shall die.
	*She moves away, then stamps the ground with her staff once more. The **Soldiers** beat on their shields. **MacRory** and **Finnleach** break their freeze and fight. **MacRory** disarms **Finnleach** and knocks him down. The **Soldiers** stop beating their shields.*
MacRory	Dost thou beg mercy from me now?
Finnleach	I do. And if thou show'st it, thou shalt have my lands And all that I possess.

20

MacRory	Why, those I have When thou art dead; and I shall have thy life, And dearer gift I cannot take from thee. So, I take it.

He strikes **Finnleach**. *The* **Soldiers** *beat once on their shields.*

So dies my enemy.

He strikes **Finnleach** *again and kills him. The* **Soldiers** *again beat once on their shields.*

MacRory	*[To the* **Soldiers***]* But his son still lives. Seek him out, hunt him down, put an end to his life. A purse of gold to the man who brings me his head.

Exit **MacRory**, *followed one-by-one by the* **Soldiers**, *on their lines.*

Soldier 1	So ends a man's life.
Soldier 2	He lies on the ground with his weapons and his name…
Soldier 3	And even that will soon leave him.
Soldier 4	He's just one among many, the numberless dead…
Soldier 5	And we're glad of his death, because it's not ours…
Soldier 6	Though ours may come tomorrow, or the next day.
Soldier 7	Until it does, hold fast onto life…
Soldier 8	While the crows gather and the wolves watch.

Gruach and the Wyrd Sisters remain onstage for the next scene.

Scene 3

Gruach	*[Raising her head from the pool]* I see nothing. Only dark water, silent stones. Haven't you heard me? Won't you answer my prayer?
	*Gruach turns back to the water. The **Wyrd Sisters** now speak to **Gruach**, but she makes no sign that she's heard them.*
Girl	We hear. And shall answer.
Goodwife	We'll grant your heart's desire.
Crone	But in our own time – and in our own way.
	*Enter **Magg** and **Grimm**, near **Finnleach**'s body. **Grimm** is carrying a bag.*
Magg	Didn't I say we'd have rich pickings from these wars, husband?
Grimm	Aye, Magg, you did. Though in my opinion –
Magg	Your opinion? What's this? Does Grimm have an opinion about something?
Grimm	Of a sort –
Magg	We'd best hear it, then.
Grimm	It ain't worth the airing –
Magg	Out with it, I say! If your brain has took the trouble to manufacture itself an opinion, then for all the pain and trouble it must've cost, I'll hear what it is. Out with it! Speak!
Grimm	Here it is, then. While I ain't denying we've made pickings enough –
Magg	And a fool you'd be to deny it, seeing as you have them pickings there in your own hands.
Grimm	So I do – and here's the thing. While these pickings might have much in the way of bulk and weight, they ain't exactly what you might call rich.
Magg	And that's your opinion, is it?

Grimm	You asked for it, Magg, and now you've heard it.
Magg	I did, and I wish I hadn't, for it's my opinion that your opinion ain't worth so much as a dog's fart. *[Turning her attention to Finnleach's corpse]* Now, here's an odour of another colour. It has the smell of wealth about it, and that's the sweetest smell there is. *[Examining the corpse]* Grimm! Come here and see!
Grimm	*[Approaching Magg]* What is it?
Magg	This golden chain about his neck! That speaks of rank and nobility. And the buckle on his belt – pure silver, and studded with gems. And here, look, upon his finger, this ring of solid gold. What a chieftain we have here, Grimm! And like a good chieftain, he'll supply his loyal subjects with rich gifts.
Grimm	His subjects? You said we serve nobody but ourselves.
Magg	We do, and in serving him, we serve ourselves.
Grimm	How shall we serve him if he's dead?
Magg	By disposing of his body, for which courtesy he'll richly reward us. Take him up.
Grimm	You mean I should carry him?
Magg	I mean you should. I'll take the bag and you take the body.
Grimm	I don't know as I care to.
Magg	What? Feared of it, are you? Does this dead lump of human meat fill you with such fright that you dare not carry him?
Grimm	I dare do all that may become a man –
Magg	Then prove you are one and take up the corpse.
	She takes the bag from Grimm, and Grimm takes hold of Finnleach's body.
Grimm	Where to?
Magg	Somewhere more private, where we can perform unobserved our most holy and solemn rites.
Grimm	Eh?

Magg
Somewhere we can strip the body unseen. It's sure enough, husband, I married you for your brawn and not your brains. Come. Follow me.

*Exit **Magg**, followed by **Grimm**, dragging **Finnleach**'s body. **Gruach** and the **Wyrd Sisters** remain onstage for the next scene.*

Scene 4

Gruach	*[Looking up]* Silent yet, and only the moon's face Shows in the water. The spirits don't hear me, Or choose not to – or perhaps no longer here, Gone from the world, so long unrecognised, They are fled and forgotten. These stones, That once upon a time did move and speak, Are stones only, all potency and power Sunk back into the earth, and there they sleep. Foolish to think I could awaken them –
Girl	Not so.
Gruach	What?
Goodwife	We are here…
Gruach	Those voices –
Crone	And your prayer will be answered.
Gruach	I hear them –
Sisters	Now!

*Enter **Thorfinn**, suddenly. He is wild and breathless. With a gasp,*
Gruach swings round to face him. He too is pulled up sharp, facing her.

Thorfinn	Help me. Please.
Gruach	Who are you?
Thorfinn	I'm Thorfinn, Finnleach's son, of the clan Macbeth.
Gruach	Why do you want my help?
Thorfinn	My life depends upon it.
Gruach	How? Tell me.
Thorfinn	My family holds lands to the west of here And, bordering ours, lie those of another, Those of Gillacomgain. For years there's been a feud between us, The reason and the cause forgotten But the passion and the hatred not.

25

Gruach	Some dispute over territory seems the likeliest cause.
Thorfinn	You know about such things?
Gruach	My family has some experience of them. Go on.
Thorfinn	In recent times, the feud once more Has erupted into violence. We gathered our followers, They gathered theirs; Where the river borders both our lands, our forces met; And, to make short of things, they won, we lost. Our people slaughtered or scattered, My father fled – to safety, I hope. Myself now fleeing too, fleeing for my life, I'm a hunted man, like a stag with the hounds Hot on my trail. All day I've been running; Now my strength is spent, I can't run further. I need a place to hide, Someone to guide me there And not reveal my whereabouts. This is what I ask – beg of you.
Gruach	You'd trust me with your life, even though you don't know me?
Thorfinn	I must. There's no one else. And there's an honesty in your face that gives me hope.
Gruach	You can be certain, if I say I'll help you, I will.
Thorfinn	I believe it. I've heard that, in olden times, This was a place of sanctuary; That dwelling here were certain guardian spirits. And though I'm a follower of the one true religion, I'm willing to put my trust in ancient powers If they can save my life.
Gruach	Trust to them, then, and also to me. On the hill's slope there's a hawthorn tree, Gnarled and twisted, its roots knotted Into the earth. Between those roots There is an opening, just wide enough

For a man to squeeze through. It goes deep
Into the hillside, where it opens out
To a hollow cave. Shelter there,
But treat the place with reverence and care,
For if these ancient spirits still abide,
That's where they have their home.

Thorfinn	Lady, I'll do as you say And if I survive, And if I ever have again the means, I'll repay this kindness.
Gruach	There'll be a time for that. Go, now, quickly, And may your God and my spirits protect you.

*Exit **Thorfinn**. **Gruach** gazes after him.*

Girl	She watches him go, into the darkness…
Goodwife	And she thinks she'll never see him again.
Crone	But she's wrong. She will.
Girl	For we've heard her prayer, and answered it…
Goodwife	And she's seen the face of her own true love…
Crone	The man she'll live for, the man she'll die for.

***Gruach** and the **Wyrd Sisters** remain onstage for the next scene.*

27

Scene 5

*Enter the **Soldiers**.*

Soldier 1	You! Girl! Turn around.
Gruach	*[Turning]* What do you want?
Soldier 2	Shut up! We ask the questions.
Soldier 3	And we're asking you now. Have you seen anybody?
Soldier 1	A man, that's who we're looking for.
Soldier 2	An outlaw, on the run.
Soldier 3	You seen anyone like that?
Gruach	I've seen no one.
Soldier 1	You sure?
Gruach	Yes.
Soldier 2	Nobody at all?
Gruach	That's right.
Soldier 3	Just been here on your own?
Gruach	Yes.
Soldier 1	And why's that, then? What's a young girl like you doing out here on her own?
Soldier 2	And at night, in a place like this?
Soldier 3	An evil place, this is. So what are you doing here?
Soldier 1	Maybe she's a witch, come here to cast a spell.
Soldier 2	No, she's too young and pretty to be a witch.
Soldier 3	That's right. Witches are old and ugly, everybody knows that.
Soldier 1	So what's she doing here, then?
Soldier 2	She's here to pray. Asking the stones to send her a man.
Soldier 3	And it looks like her prayers have been answered, lads.

*The **Soldiers** begin to close in on **Gruach**.*

Soldier 1	They have, and three times over…
Soldier 2	And she has three men instead of one…
Soldier 3	And three can have more pleasure than one –
	Enter MacRory.
MacRory	Stay! Let not one of you touch her, or his life ends here! This girl's no peasant slut to slake* your thirsts. Can't you see she's gentle-born? Fall back! About your proper business – which is, if you recall, to find Finnleach's son.
Soldier 1	He's not here, lord.
MacRory	You're certain of that?
Soldier 2	Most certain.
MacRory	And how do you know?
Soldier 3	This girl – the lady – says she's seen no one.
Soldier 1	And if he'd come this way she would have seen him.
MacRory	Unless she's lying, in which case you'd search the hilltop to make sure she wasn't. Wouldn't you?
Soldier 2	Of course, lord, yes –
MacRory	And have you?
Soldier 3	Not yet, but we were just going to –
MacRory	Then be about it! Now! Go!
	Exit the Soldiers.
MacRory	*[Turning to Gruach]* I apologise for my men. They're good for fighting, but not much else.
Gruach	No doubt for dying, too.
MacRory	No doubt of that. They know how to die.
Gruach	So do we all, when our time comes.
MacRory	But some not so well as others.
Gruach	And did they die well whom you killed today?
MacRory	How do you know I've killed?
Gruach	The blood on your hands … and the light in your eyes.

---

*   *slake – quench or satisfy*

MacRory	Some died well, some not so well. In the end it makes no difference. But it's a grim thing for us to stand here and talk of death.
Gruach	What else should we speak of?
MacRory	Your name, lady. We can speak of that.
Gruach	As we can speak of yours.
MacRory	We can and shall. My name is MacRory of the clan Gillacomgain, Lord of Moray. And yours?
Gruach	Gruach, and I have no clan.
MacRory	Gruach? That's no Christian name.
Gruach	But a name that's native to this land, which yours is not.
MacRory	How so?
Gruach	My people held this land long before yours.
MacRory	Your people? You're Pictish, then.
Gruach	And proud to be.
MacRory	Pride's all you have. You hold little enough of the land now.
Gruach	But what we have we hold dear.
MacRory	Who's your father?
Gruach	Beoedhe.
MacRory	Then I'm afraid, lady, I must hold you as my prisoner.
Gruach	Why?
MacRory	Your father's a traitor.
Gruach	He's no traitor!
MacRory	He gave support to my enemy, the man I killed today and whose son so far escapes me. And as I am a loyal subject of the king –
Gruach	My father's father was a king –
MacRory	But still I call your father traitor, and you my prisoner.
	*Enter the **Soldiers**.*
Soldier 1	We've searched everywhere and can't find him.

30

Soldier 2	Neither track nor trace.
Soldier 3	If he was here, the earth itself has swallowed him up.
MacRory	No doubt it will disgorge* him at some future time, and when he comes to light, his life is mine. Meanwhile, we have this captive: a fair prize to end a bloody day. Bring her with us. And treat her well, for she's a prize I mean to treasure and hold dear.

*Exit **Gruach**, **MacRory**, and the **Soldiers**. The **Wyrd Sisters**
remain onstage for the next scene.*

---

* *disgorge – discharge, eject (usually food) from the throat or mouth*

*Enter **Magg** and **Grimm**, **Grimm** carrying their bag of loot.
Magg has a dagger at her belt.*

Magg Set the bag down here, Grimm, and we'll count our day's takings at leisure.

Grimm Why not further off?

Magg Why not here, where I say?

Grimm I've no liking for this place.

Magg I like it well enough. It's remote, and there's no human eye to pry into our business.

Grimm No human eye, no. But there might be other kinds.

Magg Such as?

Grimm Them stones –

Magg Eh? The stones? You think them stones have eyes?

Grimm I think they have a watchful look about them.

Magg A stone's a stone, having neither organ nor sense, but being solid stone only, all the way through. A bit like your head.

*She raps **Grimm** on the head with her knuckles.*

Let's get on.

***Magg** opens the bag and takes out the loot, which includes the items they took from **Finnleach**.*

Husband, if I'm not mistook, that last chap we found has made our fortunes. The quality of this loot is most rare. Such pure gold and fine-worked silver. Some rich and powerful lord, he was. But where's all his power and riches now? His power dispersed to dust and his riches in our hands! It was a lucky day for us when he met his end. What do you say, Grimm?

Sisters *[Whispering softly, again and again, throughout the following conversation]* By the pricking of my thumbs,
Something wicked this way comes.

Magg	Grimm?
Grimm	Listen!
Magg	What?
Grimm	Can't you hear?
Magg	Hear what?
Grimm	That sound…
Magg	What sound?
Grimm	That … whispering …
Magg	Whispering?
Grimm	Voices whispering –
Magg	There ain't no voices –
Grimm	Listen!

*As they stop talking to listen, the **Sisters** stop whispering.*

Magg	I don't hear anything.
Grimm	It's stopped.
Magg	It never started. Now, back to business.

*Enter **Thorfinn**, during the following speech. **Grimm** sees him, but **Magg** does not.*

I think it best we don't carry this stuff around with us. There's some no-good folk live in these parts – ruffians and bandits the lot of them – and we don't want to get robbed and murdered, do we? So I propose we bury it here till we've found ourselves a place to live, and then come back for it piece by piece and sell it to whoever'll pay the highest price. Agreed?

Grimm is staring at Thorfinn.

Are we agreed? Grimm? What's the matter with you now? You look like you've seen a ghost.

Grimm	I think I have.
Magg	What?
Grimm	There!
Magg	There's a ghost, is there, standing behind me?

Grimm	Yes!
Magg	First it's stones with eyes, then it's whispering voices, and now it's ghosts. Husband, you've been in this land too long, and your brains have turned to porridge.
Grimm	I can see it!
Magg	There ain't nothing there –
	She turns and sees **Thorfinn**.
Grimm	You see it now?
Magg	I do.
Grimm	I know a spell my mother taught me for getting rid of ghosts. *[To* **Thorfinn***]* Aroint* thee, fiend! Foul sprite of hell and goblin damned, whate'er thou art, I abjure** thee and command thee to be gone! *[***Thorfinn*** remains still, staring at* **Grimm**. **Grimm** *turns to* **Magg***]* It didn't work.
Magg	That's cos it ain't no ghost. I've got something here'll see it off, though. *[Drawing the dagger from her belt]* Whoever you are, you'd best make tracks. I'm armed, and I know how to use this.
Thorfinn	Is that a dagger I see?
Magg	It is, and you'll be feeling it between your ribs if you come a step closer.
Thorfinn	It's my father's.
Magg	What?
Thorfinn	The dagger you're holding. It belonged to my father. I should know. I gave it to him.
Magg	Your father –
Thorfinn	Finnleach Macbeth. I'm his son, Thorfinn. *[Drawing his sword]* The last time I saw him he wore that dagger in his belt. How did you come by it? Did you rob and murder him? You must have done. He wouldn't give it up and still be living, and scum like you don't kill men in battle. Tell me! Let the last thing you both speak be the truth!

34   * *aroint – 'Begone'. Shakespearean in origin.*
    ** *abjure – solemnly discard, spurn*

Grimm	We didn't kill your father!
Thorfinn	Die with a lie on your lips, then!
Magg	My husband speaks the truth! Believe us, sir, we're no murderers! But your father is dead, and if you hear us out we'll tell you how he died.
Thorfinn	Speak, then. Be quick. My father's death must be avenged.
Magg	But not on us, for we had no hand in it. Your father died in battle. And died bravely, too.
Grimm	That's right. He stood one against three, and drove them back, but these four pressed him hard and wore him down until his strength gave out, and at last the five of them cut him down and slew him.
Thorfinn	You saw him die?
Grimm	We did –
Magg	Not. We did not. We came upon his body afterward as we were looking to help the wounded.
Thorfinn	Then how do you know how he died?
Grimm	That's plain: he told us himself.
Thorfinn	You can speak with the dead, then?
Grimm	What?
Thorfinn	You said he was slain.
Magg	So he was, and his life on the point of expiring when we found him. With his final breath he told us who he was, and commanded us to find you and tell you how he died. And to give you his most treasured possession. This dagger.
Grimm	And the chain. We have a chain of his as well.
Magg	The chain, yes. The dagger and the chain –
Grimm	And the buckle from his belt.
Magg	The dagger, the chain, and the buckle. We have them all in our safekeeping.
Thorfinn	It was fortunate I came to be here, then.

35

Magg	Fortune or fate, sir. To my way of thinking it was fate brought you here, and brought us too. We're all fate's children, and must go where she sends us.
Thorfinn	A man makes his own fate, and his own way in the world – but let that pass. I'll have my father's things.
Magg	Of course. Give me the bag, husband.

Grimm gives her the bag and she rummages through it, taking out the items and passing them to Thorfinn, as she speaks.

	I must say, sir, you've taken the news of your father's death very well. Shows nobility of spirit, that does. Strength of character. Those are good qualities in a man.
Thorfinn	There'll be a time for mourning. Tomorrow.
Magg	And tomorrow and tomorrow. It's my feeling fate has many tomorrows in store for you, when she may well deal you a better hand than she has done today. There you are, sir. Dagger, chain and buckle.
Grimm	And there's the ring.
Magg	The ring?
Thorfinn	You have my father's ring?
Grimm	We do –
Magg	We did. I can't find it here. Oh, sir, we seem to have lost it –
Grimm	No, we haven't, Magg. It's on your finger.
Magg	What? Oh, yes! I forgot. I put it there for safekeeping. Thank you for reminding me, husband. What would I do without you? *[Taking off the ring and giving it to Thorfinn]* There. Your father's ring. Now you're fit to take on the world.
Thorfinn	I wish that were so. There are scores to be settled. But not yet.
Magg	You have a plan?
Thorfinn	I'm not safe here. I must somehow make my way across the sea to Orkney. I have kin there.
Magg	For that you'll need a boat. And now you'll see how once more fate plays her hand in your favour, for it just so happens we know a man with a boat.

Grimm	We do?
Magg	We do. And I'm sure, with some persuasion, he'll hire it out. Though it will cost.
Thorfinn	I've no doubt of that.
Magg	No more delay, then. Come with us and we'll bring you to the boat.
Thorfinn	It seems I have no choice. Very well. Lead on.
Magg	It's a fair path you'll be taking, sir, and one that will lead us all to better fortunes.

They prepare to depart.

Grimm	The bag.

*Exit **Magg** and **Thorfinn**. **Grimm** takes up the bag. As he does so, the **Wyrd Sisters** begin to whisper again. He stops, looks up, sees them, stares in terror, then turns and runs off the stage. The **Sisters** come forward. In turn, each one picks up her doll and raises it.*

Sisters	So the charm's wound up
	And their tale's begun,
	And it won't be over
	Till it's done;
	And their lives are wound
	With a single thread,
	And it won't be cut
	Until they're dead.

They move back to the stones and sit, cradling their dolls. They beat on the floor with their hands, and chant.

Sound the trumpet,
Beat the drum,
Cry 'All hail':
The king doth come!

They stop beating, abruptly, and remain onstage for the next scene.

*Enter **King Malcolm**, with **MacRory** and **Duncan**, who stand on either side of him.*

Malcolm	*[To the audience]* Malcolm, king of Scotland.
Duncan	*[To the audience]* Duncan, his nephew.
MacRory	*[To the audience]* MacRory Gillacomgain, his most loyal thane.
Malcolm	Met here to settle these latest troubles, and bring peace once more to our country.
MacRory	Though till Finnleach's son is found, my mind can never be settled…
Duncan	And as long as these Picts hold land and power, the country will never know peace.
Malcolm	We intend to address that. *[Calling]* Bring the prisoners forward!

*Enter two **Soldiers**, bringing with them **Beoedhe** and **Gruach**.*

	Beoedhe, how do you answer the charge of treason?
Beoedhe	I know of no honest reason why such a charge should be made. I've never raised arms against my king.
MacRory	You gave help to the traitor Finnleach.
Beoedhe	Since when has friendship been an act of treachery? Finnleach was my friend. He asked for shelter and I gave it –
MacRory	And Finnleach was a traitor!
Beoedhe	For being your enemy?
Malcolm	For being enemy to my chosen successor. I have no children. MacRory Gillacomgain is my adopted heir.
Gruach	My father didn't know this!
Duncan	He knows it now! And would it have made any difference if he had known it before?
Beoedhe	I say again, Finnleach was my friend. I do not betray friendship.
Duncan	An admittance of guilt.

Beoedhe	These are dark days, indeed, when to be a true friend is a crime. Yet my people, more than yours, hold friendship as a sacred trust, never to be broken –
Duncan	Your people! What are your 'people'?
Beoedhe	You know well. Natives of this land and once its power –
Duncan	A power that called on demons and drank blood! Witches and devil-worshippers! Enemies of all that's holy! This man would be found guilty even if he'd led a spotless life, for by his birth he's a traitor to both king and Christ –
Gruach	Do you forget who he is? That his father was elected king in this land *[pointing at Malcolm]* and that you hold power now because of him!
Malcolm	That's not forgotten, and will be taken into account when our judgement's made.
MacRory	I wish to add my voice to this.
Malcolm	Speak. You'll be listened to.
MacRory	Beoedhe I leave to your judgement. But, as to his daughter … as it was I took her captive, let her remain captive with me for as long as her life lasts.
Malcolm	You'd be her jailor?
MacRory	I'd be her husband –
Gruach	No!
MacRory	And breed the pagan out of her blood.
Gruach	This shall not be!
Malcolm	You have no choice.
Gruach	Father!
Duncan	And his life is forfeit.
Malcolm	*[To MacRory]* There's sense and wisdom in your proposal.
Duncan	And theology. For Christ says we should love our enemies.
Malcolm	Hear my judgement. Beoedhe's daughter shall become Gillacomgain's wife. Her dowry shall be all Beoedhe's lands and properties here in Scotland. To him also shall go the lands of

the traitor Finnleach. Duncan, to you shall go Finnleach's fiefdom* of Northumberland, where you'll rule as prince.

Duncan   I thank you for that, uncle.

Malcolm   Beoedhe, for your royal father's sake, though you're judged a traitor, your sentence shall be banishment, not death.

Beoedhe   It's the same thing. To tear me from my native land is to tear my life from me.

Malcolm   That life you'll lose if, after ten days, you're found within these borders.

Duncan   And let that stand for Northumberland too.

Gruach   Do you call this judgement? Where there's judgement, there's justice to be found, and I see no justice here. Only cruel vengeance, tyranny and persecution! If I had the power –

Beoedhe   You have none. Only that which you derive from your husband.

Gruach   Father?

Beoedhe   Our people's time is past. You are all that remains. Accept what must be, and live, that some memory of them shall live in you.

MacRory   Heed what your father tells you, Gruach. Your farewells are made. Come with me, now. Obey me. I am your lord.

*Exit **Gruach**, with **MacRory**.*

Malcolm   Does this satisfy you, nephew?

Duncan   It does.

Malcolm   Then we're done here. *[To the **Soldiers**, indicating **Beoedhe**]* Take him outside. Give him food, and a cloak against the weather, and set him on his road.

Duncan   From which, for him, there'll be no looking or turning back.

*Exit **Malcolm** and **Duncan**.*

Soldier 1   *[To **Beoedhe**]* Stay there awhile. There's a matter he and I must discuss.

*Soldier 1 draws **Soldier 2** away from **Beoedhe**.*

Soldier 2   What matter's this?

Soldier 1   The matter of our duty.

40   * *fiefdom – area within a person's control or operation*

Soldier 2	Our duty's plain enough –
Soldier 1	Is it, though? 'No looking or turning back.' What do you think was meant by that?
Soldier 2	Nothing. It was a manner of speaking.
Soldier 1	That's where you're wrong. With these lords, all's veiled meanings and hidden intents. What Duncan spoke, he spoke with purpose. And, if we are to thrive, we must discover that purpose, and act upon it.
Soldier 2	And have you discovered it?
Soldier 1	I think I have. The clue's in the words. 'See to it.' There's the first clue. 'No looking back.' There's the second. How may we see to it that he may neither look nor turn?
Soldier 2	A man needs sharper eyes than mine to spy the answer to this riddle.
Soldier 1	While he needs none at all!
Soldier 2	No eyes, you mean?
Soldier 1	I do. We must deprive this old man of his sight.
Soldier 2	That's a cruel command.
Soldier 1	Greater cruelty may fall on us if we don't carry it out.
Soldier 2	Well, duty's duty, and we're only the tools of the great. Let him that gave this order have his conscience pricked, for I have none.
Soldier 1	As neither shall this one have eyes after we've pricked them.
	They turn back to **Beoedhe**.
	[To **Beoedhe***]* Our apologies for keeping you.
Beoedhe	You could keep me longer and I'd make no protest.
Soldier 2	Your welcome's outstayed and we must take you from here. Come.
Beoedhe	I fear you'll have to lead me. My eyes are blind with tears.
Soldier 1	That's an ailment we have a remedy for.
Soldier 2	And there'll be no more weeping after we've given it.
	Exit **Soldiers***, with* **Beoedhe***. The* **Wyrd Sisters** *remain onstage for the next scene.*

*Enter **Gruach**. She stands facing out over the audience as the **Wyrd Sisters** speak.*

Girl	Time's passed. See her now.
Goodwife	The girl a woman…
Crone	The daughter a wife…
Girl	But the maid still a maid.
Goodwife	That's something she holds dear and keeps close.
Crone	See the wife-maiden at the window.
Girl	It's deepest night. The moon is new.
Goodwife	All sleep. But she doesn't.
Crone	All dream. She too has dreamt.

*Enter **MacRory**. He and **Gruach** carry out the actions as now described by the **Wyrd Sisters**.*

Girl	And now … her husband –
Goodwife	Who is no husband –
Crone	He's woken, found the bed cold and empty.
Girl	But the bed's always cold and always empty.
Goodwife	He approaches. She hears him. She does not turn.
Crone	Her eyes are fixed on the moon. He speaks to her.
Sisters	Listen.
MacRory	Gruach. Why have you left our bed?
Gruach	I woke. I couldn't sleep.
MacRory	The night's cold.
Gruach	I don't feel it.
MacRory	You should try and sleep.
Gruach	Why should I?

MacRory	Sleep will ease your spirit of its ills.
Gruach	Then I pray that I'll never sleep again, And that my spirit's ills become a nest Of writhing vipers, spitting poison, and Infecting all.
MacRory	Wife –
Gruach	Never speak that name.
MacRory	You are my wife.
Gruach	And only in name.
MacRory	I'd have it so in deed.
Gruach	Then make it so. You have the strength and power to force your will.
MacRory	I'd win you with love, not force.
Gruach	*[Turning to MacRory]* Then stay unsatisfied. You banished love from me the day you banished my father.
MacRory	What if that banishment was revoked? I'll speak with the king. As I'm his heir, he'll listen, and your father shall be restored –
Gruach	If he still lives –
MacRory	I believe he does.
Gruach	You know it?
MacRory	I'm certain.
Gruach	Have you had news of him?
MacRory	Yes, and still living.
Gruach	Do then bring my father home, and I'll be your wife.
MacRory	All shall be done that can.
	MacRory puts out his hand as if to touch Gruach. She turns from him to face out over the audience again. Exit MacRory.
Girl	But she knows he's lying.
Goodwife	She knows what's happened to her father.
Crone	Her dream has shown her…

Girl	The dream that woke her…
Goodwife	The dream which waking doesn't dispel…
Crone	The dream she sees in waking still…
Girl	And lives it…
Goodwife	And breathes it…
Crone	And speaks it.

*Enter **Beoedhe**, during **Gruach**'s speech. Slowly, while speaking, **Gruach** turns to watch him.*

Gruach   I saw a man walking a track in the wild lands; dressed in rags, hunched against the weather, against the world. Slowly he walked, each step painful and stumbling, and the staff he carried knocked on the earth, as if he were seeking a place to enter. At last he came to the place of the stones. Weary, he rested there, leaned on his staff. Then he approached one, laid his hand flat against it; and he raised his head, and I saw his face, and I saw the bloody rag tied about his eyes, and I knew he was blind, and I knew he was my father.

Beoedhe   *[To the first standing stone]* What's this? Is it a man? I pray you, fair sir, alms for a poor beggar. I think you have a kind face, but I cannot tell for sure, for I have lost my eyes. How did I lose them? That I can't tell you, for I can't tell myself. At gambling, most likely. And in the same game I lost my daughter, and that's why I'm poor, for she was all the wealth I had. No words of pity or condolence? Good day to you, then, sir, and may your lungs rot.

Beoedhe moves on to the next standing stone.

Gruach   My father, blind, body broken, mind broken, too; fate's plaything, creation's wrack* and flotsam**. There, where I'd sought a husband, he sought sanctuary, and found none.

Beoedhe   *[To the second standing stone]* Spare a copper for an old soldier, mister. A couple of pennies for a pie and a pint. Stuff my gut and get roaring drunk. And why shouldn't I drown my sorrows in a cup? I've more than my share of sorrows, mate. I carry them on my back so I must stoop. And my legs ache something rotten. But I won't weep, not me. Truth is, I can't, for I don't possess the organs for it. My daughter weeps enough for both of us, though. Sometimes I think I hear her. Do you hear her? Don't the sound of it crack your stony heart? No? Curse you, then, and be gone!

He moves to the third standing stone.

Gruach   I longed to speak to him, but I could not. I longed to go to him, but I could not. I gazed as one who gazes into a deep pool, and sees within a world of horrors, and feels that horror in her heart, but cannot act upon it.

Beoedhe   *[To the third standing stone]* Are you hard-hearted like these others? Stone quite through? Wilt not give this onetime prince a purse, a crust, a kind word? The world's cruel and the wind's cold, cold and sharp. But not as sharp as the knife that cut out my eyes. Aye, thus I was used. My eyes they cut from my head, and my daughter they cut from my heart. And I know which wound has healed and which still bleeds. Dost smile? Dost mock my plight? Then 'tis like thou art the one that stole my sight! *[To the second stone]* And thou my daughter! *[To the first stone]* And thou the one that commanded both! Now I know you three for what you are! And though you may show your painted faces to the world, I see the skull that lies beneath the skin. So I'll turn blind prophet like the ancient Greek and tell

---

* *wrack – coarse brown seaweed which grows on the shoreline*
** *flotsam – the wreckage of a ship washed up by the sea*

your futures. *[Pointing with his staff at each stone in turn]* You shall die, all three. The worms shall gnaw your flesh. Your bones shall become dust in the earth. The rest is silence. I'll say no more to you. There's a grim-faced fellow here would speak with me. He has much to say. And all eternity to say it.

Beoedhe turns from the stones and faces out over the audience.

Gruach Then I tried to speak to him. In my dream I called out his name, but even as I spoke, he was gone.

Exit Beoedhe.

And then I woke, and I knew that he was dead.

*The **Wyrd Sisters** remain onstage for the next scene, as does **Gruach**, looking out.*

Scene 9

Girl	What now, sisters?
Goodwife	We wait for her to come.
Crone	And she will come, seeking vengeance…
Girl	For her father's death…
Goodwife	And her own forced marriage…
Crone	The crimes committed against kin and kind.
Girl	Will she come soon?
Goodwife	She approaches now.
Crone	A day has passed, and a night, and a day.
Girl	The sun is setting…
Goodwife	The sky blood-red…
Crone	The horns of a hunter's moon on the horizon.

Gruach moves across to the stones.

Girl	And she, the huntress, is here…
Goodwife	Seeking her weapons…
Crone	And tracking her prey.

Gruach kneels before the pool.

Gruach
If there are spirits that dwell in this place,
Let them hear me.
If there is a power lies in these stones,
Let my voice unlock it.
You powers of earth,
Of root and stone,
Of stream and leaf,
Who cause the winds to roar,
The seas to boil and churn;
You makers and unmakers of the dead,
You dread and holy guardians of the night,

Take heed my prayer.
I call you and conjure you:
Come to me now.

*The **Wyrd Sisters** speak to **Gruach**. Hearing them, she starts.*

Girl   We are here.

Goodwife   We have always been here.

Crone   Do you hear us?

Gruach   I hear you. But do not see you.

Girl   That time will come.

Goodwife   Are you content?

Gruach   I will be, when I have my desire.

Crone   What is your desire?

Gruach   Vengeance.

Girl   What's the cause?

Gruach   My father's death.

Goodwife   Who shall suffer?

Gruach   Those that sent him to it.

Crone   What's your father to us?

Gruach   To you, nothing. To me, all.

Crone   What will you give to avenge his death?

Gruach   Whatever is required, I'll give.

Girl   All is required…

Goodwife   So shall you give…

Crone   And we shall give you vengeance.

Gruach   Then I am content.

Girl   Now the price…

Goodwife   Our payment…

Crone   The thing required.

Gruach   Tell me. What must I do?

Girl	Have a child.
Goodwife	Be a good wife to your husband.
Crone	Bear him a son.
Gruach	How shall this avenge my father's death?
Girl	This son you'll raise in the old ways.
Goodwife	In him, your father shall live.
Crone	His spirit, the spirit of his people.
Girl	In him, your father shall live, and rule…
Goodwife	True king of this country…
Crone	And our spirit shall reign once more.
Gruach	But his father –
Girl	His father shall not live.
Goodwife	Vengeance shall come swift.
Crone	When your child is born, your husband shall die.

Gruach stands.

Gruach	I'll do what's required. I'll have a child, and that child shall be a son, and that son shall be a king. From this moment, my hope and my dreams rest in him.

Exit Gruach during the Wyrd Sisters' next lines.

Girl	And she goes towards her future…
Goodwife	The future we're telling…
Crone	The story we're making.
Girl	Tracks in the dirt.
Goodwife	Footprints in sand.
Crone	Uncertain paths through an uncharted landscape.
Sisters	She takes those paths, She walks ahead; Footsteps firm, And sure her tread. This virgin maid

Though newly-wed,
Who should be seeking
Love, instead,
Is seeking vengeance
For the dead;
And as she's woman
Born and bred,
She'll find it in
Her husband's bed!

*The **Wyrd Sisters** remain onstage for the next scene, sitting by the stones.*

Scene 10

*Enter **Magg**, carrying a bag.*

Magg   *[To the audience]* My husband's a fool! As if I never knew it.
Why else did I marry him? If a woman's wise, she'll marry a
fool, and the wiser the woman, the greater the fool she'll marry.
Which must make me wiser than Solomon, for there's no
greater fool in the Christian nor the Pagan world than my
husband. The only wise thing he ever did was marry me, and
that was because his mother threw him out on account she
couldn't put up with his foolishness no more. And now the
dolt's gone and spent all our loot. Everything we won from the
wars, and not a penny left. And where is it? In his gut. To be
more precise, it's down the drain; for he swilled it all down,
then threw it back up again. A sore head he had for that, from
his hangover and my fists. Then I sent him packing and told
him not to come back till he'd made some gain. Where he is
now I don't know and don't care. I have my own schemes in
mind, and they don't call for him to be a part of them. In this
here bag, I have herbs and charms, remedies for all ills – so
I call them, at any rate, to those who have belief in such things.
And now I'm known as a Wise Woman and Healer, and sell
these potions to the blessed ignorant. And I'm not just talking
about the common folk. There's them of wealth and standing
too as come seek me out. And such a one's on her way here
now. A lady of high rank, wife of some noble lord – Macduff or
Macdaft or some such name. It's a child she's after. Two years
married and her womb empty as a dried-up well. So to me she
came for help, and I've arranged to meet her here to give her
the cure I've so carefully concocted. It took me all of five
minutes. It'll cost her, of course. And being as she's wealthy,
it'll cost her dear.

*Enter **Lady Macduff**.*

Here she comes now, right on time.

Lady Macduff	Good madam, I am here as thou didst instruct, and at the time appointed. Hast thou the remedy thou promised me?
Magg	*[To the audience]* These folks of great degree like to speak this lofty language, but it don't flummox nor befuddle me. I can speak as high as the best of them. *[To **Lady Macduff**]* All hail to thee, good madam, and blessed be the fruit of thy most happy womb.
Lady Macduff	By this greeting, dost thou mean thou hast?
Magg	Forsooth, it doth, and doth not mean nought else.
Lady Macduff	I would take it, then.
Magg	I know thou wouldst – as I would have my payment.
Lady Macduff	*[Holding out a small bag]* Thou shalt find in here the sum that we agreed. Wouldst count it?
Magg	Nay, madam. I'll trust thy word. *[Producing a small bottle from her bag]* And here for thee is this.
Lady Macduff	This is the charm?
Magg	Nay, madam, 'tis no charm. Dost take me for a country peddler?
Lady Macduff	Why no –
Magg	Then, pray you, speak not as if thou dost.
Lady Macduff	I'm heartily sorry to have offended thee.
Magg	There's no offence, my lady. But, as thou hast thy high office, so must I have mine, and it shall not be gainsaid*.
Lady Macduff	Thou shalt find in me no opposition to thy office.
Magg	Then all's well and so it shall end. Take thou this bottle and drink the contents at one draught**. Though it be small in quantity, thou canst be assured it shall make thee large.
Lady Macduff	Thou art certain of this?
Magg	My lady, I know my business and my craft.
Lady Macduff	I do not doubt it.
Magg	Then God speed thee to thy husband's bed and a fruitful coupling –

52   *   *gainsaid – denied or contradicted, opposed*
    **   *draught – a single act of drinking (or inhaling)*

Lady Macduff	A word concerning him.
Magg	Aye?
Lady Macduff	I'd not have him know of this. My husband hath a pious nature, righteous in all matters of religion, a most devout God-fearing man, and would be moved to anger should he learn I'd ought to do with charms –
Magg	Madam, thou hast offended me! Did I not tell thee this is no charm? And think'st thou I'd have ought to do with devils, or with goblins damned? Why, I am as good a Christian soul as ever prayed in church o' Sundays. And therein lies the drug's authority.
Lady Macduff	How so?
Magg	In prayer. Before thou drink'st, thou needs must pray – a dozen Aves and Our Fathers and Hail Marys each – and make confession, and kneel in vigil through the night, bending thy thoughts and words to blessed Saint Mary the Virgin that thou art pure and chaste in heart as she. For only if thou art so shall the liquid have efficacy and worth.
Lady Macduff	I am sure I am –
Magg	Then hail and rejoice, for thou shalt get with child. Go, now, my lady, and all good fortunes go with thee.
Lady Macduff	I thank thee, good woman. Fare thee well.
	*Exit **Lady Macduff**.*
Magg	Her belly may grow big … with wind. And she may issue forth an howling fart, though I doubt it'll live long nor give her much in the way of pleasure, unless she has a nose for odours. And if she comes complaining, I'll just tell her it's plain she wasn't pure, and there it'll rest. Ain't superstition a marvellous thing? Long may religion thrive! For as long as it does, so will the likes of me.
	*Exit **Magg**. The **Wyrd Sisters** remain onstage for the next scene.*

*Enter **Grimm**.*

Grimm   What a fury is my missus when her's roused! What a raging witch of a woman! I'd sooner face all the howling damned of hell than face her in her wrath! So, by her command – which has to be obeyed, or else – I must fill my pockets and enlarge myself. That task I've been engaged in this past year, and still have nought to show for it, for the country seems starved of all but beggars and constables, and taking a crust from one's not worth the beating you get from the other. But I think my luck has changed at last. Here's an army camped, fresh-landed, with ships drawn up, and tents, and gear – and where there's soldiers, there's pickings to be had. So I'll creep around and see what's to be seen, and when I've done I'll go seek out Magg and bring her here – and pray that there's a war, for he's the lad that feeds the likes of us.

*Exit **Grimm**. Enter **Thorfinn**, now called **Macbeth**.*

Macbeth   Once more my feet tread on this native earth
Where I was born, and which I've come to claim
With flame and sword. My men are armed
And ripe for war, which soon shall be unleashed
To rock this juggling world; then vengeance howl
Throughout the stormy skies, until that man
Who killed my father falls beneath my blade:
So falls his spirit down to deepest hell.
Come, Furies*! Shake your venomed serpent locks,
And gaze with bloody looks upon my cause!
For I'll not rest until this deed is done,
Nor sheathe my rage until the battle's won!

*Enter a **Messenger**.*

Who's that?

Messenger   I come from Duncan, king of Northumberland.

Macbeth   With what request?

 *   *Furies – in Greek and Roman religion and mythology, the three daughters of Mother Earth. They were often represented as women with wings and serpent hair*

Messenger	To speak with you – if you're Macbeth.
Macbeth	I am. Where does King Duncan lie?
Messenger	With his guard, upon the cliff top there.
Macbeth	So close? I'll speak with him … and await him here.
Messenger	Very well –
Macbeth	And tell him also, if he comes in peace, he has nothing to fear.
Messenger	I'll tell him, and set his mind at ease.
	*Exit **Messenger**.*
Macbeth	*[Calling]* Captain!
	*Enter a **Captain**.*
Captain	My lord.
Macbeth	Rouse our men. Tell them to take up arms.
Captain	Do we fight?
Macbeth	Perhaps. We must stand prepared.
Captain	Our men are prepared even in their sleep. Born and bred for fighting, they are – and for dying too. They'll not let you down.
Macbeth	I know it. Go and give the command.
Captain	It's my pleasure to, my lord –
Macbeth	But they fight only on my word, Captain. Have them understand that.
Captain	I will. On your word only, my lord.
	*Exit **Captain**.*
Macbeth	Command the tide to turn, quench lightning's fire,
	Quiet the roaring wind; as easy to do that
	As hold these Norsemen back from battle.
	Duncan, if you mean ill, you'll pay the price:
	Nobility and rank mean nought to these,
	Bred and engendered in the she-bear's womb,
	And suckled on the venom of a snake.
	*Enter **Duncan**.*

	What brings you here so soon?
Duncan	Your landing was looked for and reported.
Macbeth	I've no quarrel with you, nor with your uncle.
Duncan	Why come so warlike, then?
Macbeth	To claim what's mine by right – my lands, stolen by the murderer Gillacomgain.
Duncan	Those lands were given to him by the king.
Macbeth	Then they'll be returned to me when Gillacomgain's dead.
Duncan	You mean to kill him?
Macbeth	He killed my father.
Duncan	Then you'll be declared a traitor, as was he.
Macbeth	How so? I bear arms only in this feud –
Duncan	But he you bear arms against is named a king.
Macbeth	How say you?
Duncan	My uncle's successor, heir to the throne.
Macbeth	Gillacomgain's to be king?
Duncan	Named so by Malcolm, who will with arms his adopted son support.
Macbeth	Then let it be. I'll not turn back. I have my cause –
Duncan	And I have mine, which touches on your own –

*Enter **Northmen 1** and **2**, holding **Grimm**, who is struggling to break free.*

Grimm	Let me go!
Northman 1	Keep still.
Grimm	Loose me!
Northman 2	And shut up!
Grimm	I won't –
Northman 1	Yes, you will.

Northman 1 hits Grimm.

Grimm	He hit me!
Northman 2	And so do I.
	Northman 2 hits Grimm.
Macbeth	What's this?
Northman 1	Some creature we caught prowling round the tents.
Northman 2	Up to no good –
Grimm	I've done nothing wrong!
Northman 1	Only because we caught thee before thou couldst.
Northman 2	Probably bent on stealing something…
Northman 1	Or cutting someone's throat.
Grimm	I ain't no thief nor cut-throat. I'm an honest man –
Northman 2	As ever sold his mother for a jug of ale.
Grimm	You're a liar!
Duncan	Bring him here. Let us see this honest man's face.
	The Northmen drag Grimm over to Duncan and Macbeth. Duncan takes Grimm's face in his hands and examines it.
	It's certainly not a handsome face. Nor sweet-smelling. *[To Macbeth]* Do you see honesty there?
Macbeth	I see deceit, treachery, a mean spirit, a grasping nature, a tongue that lies, a murderous heart – all this and more, but no honesty. *[To the Northmen]* Hang him.
Grimm	I've committed no crime!
Macbeth	Hang him for the crimes he would commit if he were to live. Take him away.
	The Northmen start to drag Grimm off.
Northman 1	Come on. There's a good strong rope waiting for thee –
Grimm	You can't hang me! It ain't fair!
Northman 2	I know. That's life. Very unfair.
Grimm	I saved his life!
Northman 1	Shut up.

Northman 2	Save thy squawking for the noose –
Macbeth	Wait. What was that you said? You saved my life?
Grimm	I did, only you don't remember. Or maybe you choose not to –
Macbeth	Let me see his face again.

*The **Northmen** bring **Grimm** back to **Macbeth**.*

Grimm	On the run, you was, then, and needed a boat. And where was it you come to find one? To me and my missus –
Macbeth	I remember –
Duncan	He speaks the truth, then.
Macbeth	Yes. I owe him my life. Though I paid handsomely for it.
Grimm	Boats and lives don't come cheap.
Duncan	Some lives don't. But as to yours –
Grimm	It may be nought to you, sir, but it's all I have stands between me and damnation.
Duncan	Are you damned, then?
Grimm	Ain't I a man? And ain't all men born damned?
Macbeth	But they need not die so.
Grimm	Don't you believe it. That's a tale put about by priests to keep their churches and their bellies full. Damned we're born and damned we die, and in between we dance the devil's jig.
Duncan	He damns himself. Hang him for his blasphemous words –
Macbeth	No. There's a debt to be paid. *[To **Grimm**]* You may keep your life. But I'll keep you with me.
Grimm	As a soldier, you mean? You harm yourself and me in doing that. I don't have the fighting spirit, you see, and apart from that I have bad legs –
Macbeth	You're fit enough to die as any man! *[To the **Northmen**]* Take him. Give him food and fresh clothing. And see that he remains with us.
Northman 1	We'll make sure of it.

Northman 2	Come on.
	*They take **Grimm** off.*
Duncan	That man won't make a soldier. Such as he have no loyalty nor conscience beyond what fills their stomach and their purse.
Macbeth	I know it. Safer then to keep him close and buy his service with scraps. His kind has its uses. We were speaking of your cause –
Duncan	And we'll speak further, but not here.
Macbeth	We'll go to my tent. There's something in your voice that makes me eager to hear more.
	*Exit **Macbeth** and **Duncan**. The **Wyrd Sisters** remain onstage for the next scene.*

*Enter **Gruach**, carrying her son.*

Gruach   All's still,
Midnight black and silent,
No moon or stars.
Thick cloud covers them;
Why do they hide their faces from the world?
What horror comes they'll not be witness to?
My child, you lie here in my arms,
Quiet and peaceful,
And your eyes seem wise and sad beyond your age.
What knowledge of the world
Did you bring with you from my womb?
Do you know that I desire your father's death?
And I think that death comes soon.
When I was young my mother told a tale
Of a creature that lived beneath a lake;
And it would rise
And drag its heavy footsteps across the earth,
Seeking murder in men's homes.
I seem to hear those footsteps now,
And they fill me with horror and with joy
Because I woke the beast they bring;
And when it strikes,
I fear it will strike deep.

*Enter a **Servant**.*

Servant   My lady, my apologies for disturbing you.

Gruach   It is no matter. I was not sleeping. What is your news?

Servant   Your husband has returned.

Gruach   At this hour?

Servant   The king is with him.

Gruach   The king? Here? Something stirs –

Servant	And others are expected.
Gruach	Others? What others?
Servant	I can't say. But your husband would have you greet the king –
Gruach	Say I'm not – say our child is not well, that I'll come when I'm able. You understand me?
Servant	Yes, my lady.
Gruach	Go, then. Report my words.
Servant	I will.

*Exit **Servant**.*

Gruach I ail, it's true,
And he is the sickness
Which must be cured.
I think the Sisters work their magic now:
The night air's potent with their charms and spells,
Deep as a heartbeat,
Thick as hot blood,
And their whispered voices, soft as death's-head wings⋆,
Flutter in my veins.
The dark's wound tight;
When day comes, let it rise with bloody light.

*Exit **Gruach**. The **Wyrd Sisters** remain onstage for the next scene.*

⋆   *Death-head wings – the wings of a death's head hawkmoth, a large moth which has a skull-like marking on its body*

Scene 13

Sisters	*[Chanting]* Listen!

Death's approaching;
Listen!
A sigh through the grass,
A rattle in the leaves,
Death is coming.
She comes swift;
She comes like an owl on silent wings;
Her cry stops your heart and freezes your blood.
She comes silent;
She comes like a wildcat creeping in through the window;
She squats on your chest, sucks the breath from your mouth.
She comes raging;
She comes on horseback with iron hoof beats;
Drumming your grave up out of the ground.

She's the beggar at the door,
She's the bloodstain on the floor,
She's the stranger in your bed,
She's the fever in your head.
She's the poison on the dart,
She's the worm inside your heart,
She's the body in the sack,
She's the weight upon your back.
She's the sting inside the flower,
She's the chiming of the hour,
She's the tolling of the bell,
She's the ferryman to hell.

And you pay the price,
And the price is all:
She is Queen of this world.

* Lines may be spoken individually or in chorus.

And she's here!
Let her in,
Let her in,
LET HER IN!

*The **Wyrd Sisters** remain onstage for the next scene.*

Enter Grimm.

Grimm   *[To the audience]* And it was me that did it. I let Death in and this is how it happened. There we all were, the whole army, outside this big castle, and it looked like there was going to be some kind of big battle as soon as the sun come up. And just as I was trying to work out how I might get away, them two soldiers come along again and took me off to see Macbeth and Duncan.

Enter Macbeth and Duncan.

Macbeth   *[To Grimm]* You have your life. Do you wish to add to it?

Grimm   Would that be in terms of years, sir, or in terms of hard cash?

Macbeth   Both – if you obey your orders without question.

Grimm   Oh, I'm good at doing that, sir. My wife, Magg, she trained me to it very well.

Duncan   Then come with us. And keep your mouth shut.

Grimm   *[To the audience]* So in we went and there to greet us come this other feller, MacRory Something-or-Other, the bloke who owned the castle, and none other but King Malcolm himself...

Enter Malcolm and MacRory. Duncan and Macbeth kneel in turn before Malcolm and rise as Grimm continues.

[To the audience] And when they'd all done with the greetings and meetings, off we went to this chamber inside one of the buildings; and at the doorway, Macbeth turned to me and said –

Macbeth   Guard the door. See that no one enters.

Grimm   There's no one'll get past me, sir.

Macbeth   I believe it.

Grimm   *[To the audience]* And then Duncan, he said to me, all quiet like, so only I could hear –

Duncan   And let no one out.

Grimm	*[To the audience]* Which I didn't get the meaning of till later. So, in they went and there I stood, and though they was in and I was out, and though that door was big and heavy, it had a wide keyhole, and so I heard every word they said.

Grimm watches as the meeting takes place.

Malcolm	We're met here in my son's home at the request of my nephew. Duncan, reveal your purpose.
Duncan	To settle matters between these warlike lords, and conclude a lasting peace.
MacRory	While Thorfinn remains living upon my lands, there can never be peace.
Macbeth	And there can never be peace while Gillacomgain holds the lands that are mine by right.
Malcolm	By which right?
Macbeth	The right of my clan, Macbeth, whose name I now wear.
MacRory	Hear me, Macbeth: that name you wear is treason, and a traitor's only right is death.
Macbeth	I'm no traitor. It's justice I seek –
MacRory	And you'll find it on a sword's edge –
Macbeth	As my father did, slain by your hand –
MacRory	I'll not deny it.
Macbeth	And you'll not deny my right for vengeance!
Malcolm	Macbeth, take care! If you pursue that right against my adopted son, then know you'll earn my enmity and hate.

Macbeth	I've no desire for that. I spoke in heat. I retract those words…
Duncan	As he retracts his claim for vengeance, which, as you know, uncle, is his right. He wishes only to reclaim those lands kept by his father, where he'll live in peace, a loyal subject to the king.
MacRory	This is what he says. But how do we know he'll keep his word?
Duncan	Because my word says he will. And that should be enough.
Malcolm	It is, nephew. Macbeth, your lands will be returned to you if you renounce your right to vengeance, and swear loyalty to me –
Macbeth	I do renounce that claim, and swear loyalty and allegiance to my king –
Malcolm	And to your king's heir – MacRory Gillacomgain.
Macbeth	Swear allegiance to the man who killed my father?
MacRory	To the man who slew a traitor.
Malcolm	These are my conditions for the peace.
Duncan	Macbeth, it must be done.
Macbeth	Then it shall. Gillacomgain, I pledge you my sword.
Duncan	As I, uncle, pledge you mine.

Duncan and *Macbeth* draw their swords. *Duncan, Macbeth, MacRory* and *Malcolm* freeze.

| **Grimm** | *[To the audience]* And it was like everything stopped for a minute. I seen them there with their swords drawn, and I knew what they was going to do, and why I was there to guard the door. For I'd let Death in, and I wasn't going to let her out again till I was give the word! |

*Enter **Gruach**, wearing a mask of Death.*

| **Sisters** | *[Chanting softly]* She's the beggar at the door, She's the bloodstain on the floor, She's the stranger in your bed, She's the fever in your head. |
| **Grimm** | *[To the audience]* Macbeth raised his sword. Duncan raised his. The other two stared like they couldn't believe it. |

*Gruach makes her way to stand between **Malcolm** and **MacRory**.*

Sisters	*[Chanting softly]* She's the poison on the dart, She's the worm inside your heart, She's the body in the sack, She's the weight upon your back.
Grimm	*[To the audience]* And one tried to draw his sword, and the other run for the door. But the one with the sword stumbled and fell back, and the one at the door couldn't get out.
	*Gruach raises her hands to rest them on the heads of **Malcolm** and **MacRory**.*
Sisters	*[Chanting softly]* She's the sting inside the flower, She's the chiming of the hour, She's the tolling of the bell, She's the ferryman to hell.
Grimm	*[To the audience]* Then one stabbed his sword in and out and in again, over and over, and the other was hacking away with his blade like he was chopping wood, and there was no sound, only blood everywhere, and at last them two bodies lying butchered like so much raw meat on the floor.
Gruach	And you pay the price, And the price is all: She is Queen of this world.
	*Exit **Malcolm** and **MacRory**, separately.*
Grimm	*[To the audience]* And then all hell broke loose, and I dived for cover!
	*Exit **Grimm**, running, as **Macbeth** and **Duncan** raise their swords.*
Duncan	*[Crying out]* Open the gates!
Macbeth	*[Crying out]* Break the walls!
Duncan	*[Crying out]* Put the castle to fire!
Macbeth	*[Crying out]* And kill all you find!
	*Exit **Duncan** and **Macbeth**. **Gruach** removes the mask of Death.*
Gruach	I heard the screaming, and couldn't tell if it was animal or human. It seemed to be both animal and human, coming from everywhere, screams of terror, screams of pain. I looked out

from the window of the tower. Below me people were running, some killing, some dying. Men, women, children: slaughtered as I watched. And the flames rising about them, buildings crashing into the flames, clouds of smoke billowing, thickening the light. And it went on. And it was no dream. I looked and could not look away. This was my word made flesh, this horror my prayer. This was the vengeance I had called down.

*Enter **Nurse**, carrying **Gruach's child**.*

Nurse My lady, you must fly – you and your child – your husband's killed – the king too – Duncan, his own nephew slew him, and has taken his crown –

Gruach Who killed my husband?

Nurse The other one, that was an outlaw, and calls himself Macbeth – he brought wild Northmen with him – savage wolves, they are, blood-drinkers – and now he gives them leave to burn and loot and kill – and they will kill you, my lady, you and your child – me too, the three of us, if we don't go now!

Gruach Give him to me.

*The **Nurse** gives the child to **Gruach**.*

Nurse I've wrapped him up warm – you must put on a cloak as well – against the weather and discovery – there's a gate in the wall – I'll show you where it is – it leads to a track through the woods – an ancient track, it's not widely-known – we can escape that way – and after that, who knows? – hard times ahead of us, I'm sure, but better hard times and living than a cruel death here – and if we put out trust in God –

Gruach Take him.

Nurse My lady?

Gruach If I leave, they'll pursue me, hunt us down. If I stay, there's a chance we both shall live.

Nurse Where shall I take him?

Gruach Away from here! Treat him as your own – but see that he knows who his mother is, and that one day she'll come for him.

Nurse	I wish you'd change your mind, my lady –
Gruach	I am resolved. It's better this way. Quickly, now. Take him. *[Giving the child to the **Nurse**]* Not a word to me. Go.
	*The **Nurse** starts to leave.*
	Wait! Let me see him once more –
Nurse	I don't think –
Gruach	You're right. There's no time. Take him, now.
	***Gruach** turns away from the audience. The **Nurse** takes a few turns of the stage, then stops.*
Nurse	*[To the audience]* So we stole away, amid all the killing and the slaughter, the smoke and the flame, stole away into the wild forest, and it was just like the angels of the good Lord were protecting us, for nobody saw us go and nobody came after us. And though it was dark in the forest, and beasts prowled and the wind howled, I held the child close and hurried on my way. And it was just like out of the old fairy-tales, and that gave me

comfort, for in those old tales, whatever else happens, they always come to a happy ending. And that's how I thought it would be, until I heard the wolves howling.

Exit **Nurse**, *with the child. Enter* **Macbeth**, *bloody and with sword drawn.*

Macbeth	*[To Gruach]* Are you Gillacomgain's wife?
Gruach	I am.
Macbeth	Turn. Let me see your face.

Gruach turns to face **Macbeth**.

Gruach	You know me.
Macbeth	I do.
Gruach	Much has happened since our last meeting.
Macbeth	It has.
Gruach	Many trials and sorrows for us both.
Macbeth	Indeed. That's true.
Gruach	Is that my husband's blood on your hands?
Macbeth	Amongst others'.
Gruach	Then let me kiss those hands For they're the hands of my deliverer.

Gruach kisses **Macbeth**'s *hands.*

Macbeth	I came here to kill you…
Gruach	Before you knew me. My father was your father's friend. For his sake, he was banished, died an outlaw's death; Myself forced into a hated marriage; Suffered, endured it, praying only for the day When vengeance would come. Now that day has come, And though it strikes with brutal force, Unrestrained and merciless, And though the innocent fall, I'll not fear, but welcome it.

For those two men you killed,
My husband and the king,
They were my deepest enemies,
And their blood tastes like honey on my lips.

Macbeth You and I, I think, are of one kind.

Gruach When we first met by the stones I knew it.

Macbeth I haven't forgotten the promise I made
To repay the kindness you showed me then.
Yet there's word of a child,
And I've made a vow
That none of Gillacomgain's blood shall live…

Gruach There was a child.
It's dead.
A fever took it.
And though I wept as a mother should,
I don't mourn now.
My heart's filled with rejoicing for his father's death.
So I am free of husband and child both –
But am a woman, and alone,
And in need of a protector in these unsafe times.

Macbeth	You have one in me. I promise
	No harm shall come to you.

Gruach   And I promise you that in me you shall find
A loyal, true, and most loving friend.

Macbeth   That love shall be returned.
Come with me, now. There's business still in hand.
This whole castle shall be razed to the ground,
Its timbers' ashes lost upon the wind,
No trace or remnant to be found;
Then peace restored, and Duncan proclaimed king throughout
the land.

Exit **Macbeth** *and* **Gruach**. *The* **Wyrd Sisters** *remain onstage for
the next scene.*

Scene 15

*Enter **Northmen 1, 2 and 3**, with the **Captain***.

Northman 1 So what's this all about, Captain?

Northman 2 We're being paid off?

Northman 3 Sent home?

Captain That's about the sum of it, lads.

Northman 1 It ain't fair. It ain't right! Do you call it fair?

Northman 2 I don't call it fair nor right.

Northman 3 He promised us plunder. All the loot we could take and carry.

Northman 1 And what have we done? Burn one lousy castle and kill a few peasants.

Northman 2 Hardly enough to get your blood up.

Northman 3 Hardly enough to fill your pockets.

Northman 1 Now it's 'Bye-bye, lads. Thanks for the ride, but you ain't needed no more'.

Northman 2 It's plunder we came for and plunder we'll have!

Northman 3 So let's take what's owing to us!

Captain Hold on there, lads. Take it easy. There's not enough of us. Not yet. So let's sail back and bide our time. Trouble breeds trouble, and there's more'll come of this. And when it does, we'll persuade our king to pounce, come back with fuller force, and then, like wolves, we'll hunt the country wide, and all shall flee before us – and all fall.

*Exit **Northmen** and the **Captain**. The **Wyrd Sisters** remain onstage for the next scene.*

Enter Magg, carrying Gruach's child.

Magg   *[To the audience]* Look what I got here! A baby! That's right, a little baby boy. It ain't mine, of course. I'm too old for that kind of nonsense. I found it. Found it in the forest just now. The things that turn up, eh, when you least expect them. There I was, searching for herbs and roots for my remedies, and what do I find instead? A baby. Stuck up in the branches of a tree! What was a baby doing stuck up in the branches of a tree in the middle of a forest? I mean, it didn't come there by itself, did it? So who put it there? Its mother? What kind of mother sticks a baby in a tree and leaves it there? And if it wasn't its mother, who was it? I don't know any more than you do, and I reckon it's a mystery I'll never fathom. I couldn't leave it there, could I? Even old Magg ain't that hard-hearted. So here I am with this baby, and what am I going to do with it? I ain't in the baby-raising game. But the baby-trading game, now that's a different kind of game entire, and one that I'm well-suited and well-placed for. And as luck would have it, I knows a certain lady who most earnestly desires a child, and a boy-child at that – and will, I'm certain, pay most handsome for one that's ready-made, such as heaven has dropped here in my arms! I mean Mrs Macdim, who, like the well-bred and considerate lady that she is, always arrives just on time. As she does now.

Enter Lady Macduff.

Lady Macduff   Thou hast the child?

Magg   I do – I dost, lady. 'Tis here, swaddled in my arms.

Lady Macduff   Let me see.

Magg shows her the child.

Sweet infant. Why thou art true heaven's gift, for thy countenance shines with the bright light of paradise. Where did'st thou acquire him?

Magg	Why, 'twas nearer to heaven than we stand now.
Lady Macduff	Nay, but tell me –
Magg	By your leave, good lady, that I shall not, for if thou knowest, then thou shalt have cognisance* of his origin, and 'twere best his genesis** begins with thee. Think that he truly came to thee from heaven, so shalt thou consider him as truly thine.
Lady Macduff	I would he were. If thy remedy had proved good –
Magg	If thou had proved more virtuous –
Lady Macduff	No more of that. Let me see his face again. *[Looking at the child]* Shall my husband believe truly that the child is his?
Magg	Why should he believe otherwise if thou say'st so? Is he away from home?
Lady Macduff	Aye, gone to see the new king crowned.
Magg	Present him with the child when he returns. Say thy prayers have at last born fruit, and that he has a son.
Lady Macduff	Which is no lie –
Magg	Exactly so –
Lady Macduff	And therefore no deception –
Magg	'Tis bible-truth…
Lady Macduff	And he does have something of my husband about him –
Magg	'Tis the very image.
Lady Macduff	God be praised for this miracle. And thou for being His willing instrument. *[Handing **Magg** a bag of money]* Here's payment for thy pains.
Magg	*[Handing the child to **Lady Macduff**]* And here's thy child – though thou had'st none in getting him.
Lady Macduff	My tender child – for mine thou truly art, If not of my own flesh, then of my heart. *[To **Magg**]* Our business is concluded. From this day forward, I'll see thee no more.
	*Exit **Lady Macduff**, with the child.*

---

* *cognisance – knowledge, awareness*
** *genesis – the origin or formation of something*

Magg

It's a deal that suits us both. And may good fortune go with you, dear lady, for it goes with me well enough, and with my husband, too. He has employment as gatekeeper for this Lord Macbeth, who's a good friend to the new king; so maybe he ain't such a fool as I thought, which is a rare thing, for it's a world of fools we walk in, who fret themselves with shouting sound and fury, and it'd be a strutting idiot who made no profit from it.

Exit **Magg**. *The* **Wyrd Sisters** *remain onstage for the next scene.*

Scene 17

Girl	The world's still now…
Goodwife	After the fury, the terrible calm…
Crone	The eyes gazing blank, that have seen too much…
Girl	The hands hanging loose, that have done too much…
Goodwife	The tongue silent, the brain numb…
Crone	The body slumped like old clothes on a chair.
Girl	All are sleeping.
Goodwife	The world sleeps, healing its wounds.
Crone	The dead in the earth are being forgotten…
Girl	They are becoming earth, forgetting themselves…
Goodwife	Forgetting the sun, forgetting the wind…
Crone	Forgetting that they ever lived.
Girl	All sleep, all dream…
Goodwife	Even the dead dream…
Crone	But she does not dream.

*Enter **Gruach**, now called **Lady Macbeth**. She stands staring out over the audience.*

Girl	She does not sleep.
Goodwife	She does not rest.
Crone	The dead will give her no rest.
Lady Macbeth	Much blood has been spilled, but there must be more yet. Two accounted for, one remains. These hands are still not red enough.
Girl	She, who is now the great Lady Macbeth…
Goodwife	Good wife to the powerful Lord Macbeth…
Crone	Who is loyal and trusted friend to the king.

Lady Macbeth	But he must die. This Duncan must die. If not, then my father's death goes unavenged. His blood cries out and will not give me rest.
	Enter Beoedhe's Ghost.
Beoedhe	Gruach.
Lady Macbeth	What?
Girl	She hears a voice…
Beoedhe	Daughter.
Girl	Who is it?
Goodwife	A voice in the dark…
Beoedhe	Hear me.
Crone	Her father's voice speaking to her.
Lady Macbeth	Father? Is it you?
Beoedhe	Do not forget me.
Lady Macbeth	I never shall.
Beoedhe	My spirit has no peace.
Lady Macbeth	Neither has mine.
Beoedhe	Daughter, avenge my death.
Lady Macbeth	Father, I shall.
Beoedhe	Swear.
Lady Macbeth	I do.
Beoedhe	Swear.
Lady Macbeth	With all my heart.
Beoedhe	Swear.
Lady Macbeth	By all that's sacred, I do swear.
	Exit Beoedhe's Ghost.
Girl	And her father's spirit…
Lady Macbeth	Wait!
Goodwife	The spirit that we conjured out of air and light…

Lady Macbeth	Speak with me!
Crone	Fades once more into air and light…
Lady Macbeth	Stay!
Girl	And he's gone…
Goodwife	And the sun's rising…
Crone	And the world's stirring out of its dreams.
Lady Macbeth	Duncan shall die. But he's my husband's friend… Macbeth has sworn loyalty and love… Oaths have been broken before now and men have lived, their consciences intact. But he's a king, wears authority's crown… Kings have been killed before now, and the sky's not split nor graves gaped. And though he wears the world's crown, though he be creation's king, I'll have him dragged from his celestial throne and run his very blood to earth. Only then shall the earth and I be satisfied. Only then shall my lost child be found. Only then shall I find peace.
Girl	So it's spoken…
Goodwife	And spoken, happens…
Crone	And we, the tellers, tell how it happens.
	*The **Wyrd Sisters** and **Gruach** remain onstage for the next scene.*

Scene 18

*Enter **Soldiers** 1, 2, 3 and 4, addressing the audience.*

Soldier 1	Rebellion in the West!
Soldier 2	Invaders from the North!
Soldier 3	Bloody revolt!
Soldier 4	Turmoil and strife!
Soldier 1	The land on fire!
Soldier 2	The drum of war!
Soldier 3	Our wounded country…
Soldier 4	Bleeds once more!
Soldier 1	Battle-shout.

Soldier 2	War-cry.
Soldier 3	Swords clash.
Soldier 4	Men die.
Sisters	Enter Macbeth!
	*Enter **Macbeth**. He takes up a position centre stage; the **Soldiers** stand either side of him.*
Girl	Macbeth, the hero of this conflict…
Goodwife	He quells the rebellion, drives back the invaders…
Crone	His country's saviour, his king's champion…
Soldier 1	Brave Macbeth!
Soldier 2	Valour's minion*!
Soldier 3	Worthy gentleman!
Soldier 4	Valiant cousin!
All	All hail Macbeth!
	*Exit **Soldiers**.*
Girl	*[To **Macbeth**]* All hail!
Goodwife	*[To the audience]* So riding homeward from the battle…
Crone	*[To **Macbeth**]* All hail!
Girl	*[To the audience]* Upon a waste and blasted heath…
Goodwife	*[To **Macbeth**]* All hail!
Crone	*[To the audience]* His way is stopped by…
Macbeth	*[To the **Sisters**]* Secret, black, and midnight hags!
Girl	Who greet him thus…
Sisters	Thou shalt be king hereafter!
Goodwife	And the worm's in his heart…
Crone	And begins to bite.
Macbeth	*[Turning to **Lady Macbeth**]* My dearest love, Duncan comes here tonight.
Girl	Immediately she knows his mind…

---

*   *minion – a servant or unimportant underling of a powerful person*

Lady Macbeth	He that's coming must be provided for.
Goodwife	Knows his human frailty and fear…
Macbeth	I am his kinsman and his subject.
Crone	Knows too the power that works him to her will…
Lady Macbeth	You Spirits that tend on mortal thoughts!
Girl	And when he weakens…
Macbeth	He hath honoured of late –
Goodwife	Then she's ready…
Lady Macbeth	Art thou afeared?
Macbeth	I dare do all that may become a man!
Lady Macbeth	We'll not fail!

Lady Macbeth takes a dagger from her belt and holds it up.

But screw your courage to the sticking-place.

Hesitantly, Macbeth takes the dagger.

Crone	And her will proves the stronger.
Lady Macbeth	Leave all the rest to me.

Enter Duncan. He stands apart from the Macbeths, facing out over the audience.

Duncan	This castle hath a pleasant air.
Sisters	*[Chanting]* The guest arrives, They lock the gate…
Duncan	We are your guest tonight.
Sisters	*[Chanting]* The sun has set, The hour is late…
Duncan	Conduct me to mine host.
Sisters	*[Chanting]* Darkness strikes The midnight bell…
Duncan	We love him highly.
Sisters	*[Chanting]* Their guest is sleeping, All is well.

Macbeth	I go and it is done.
	Macbeth turns to *Duncan*.
Sisters	*[Chanting]* A trembling foot Treads on the stair…
Macbeth	Hear not my steps which way they walk.
Sisters	*[Chanting]* A shiver whispers Through the air…
Macbeth	Hear it not, Duncan.
Sisters	*[Chanting]* A trembling hand Opens the door…
Macbeth	It is a bloody business.
Sisters	*[Chanting]* A shadow falls Across the floor.
	Macbeth stands behind *Duncan*, *the dagger raised in his hands as if to bring it down.*
Lady Macbeth	He is about it.
Sisters	*[Chanting]* In the dark, An owl's cry…
Lady Macbeth	The grooms do sleep.
Sisters	*[Chanting]* In the dark, A man must die…
Lady Macbeth	I laid their daggers ready.
Sisters	*[Chanting]* A candle burns, Sharp as a spike…
Lady Macbeth	Had he not resembled my father –
Sisters	*[Chanting]* An owl cries, A killer strikes!
	Macbeth brings down the dagger sharply behind *Duncan* as if stabbing him.
Duncan	*[Crying out]* Sleep no more!
Macbeth	I heard a voice!

Lady Macbeth	It was the owl.
Duncan	Macbeth hath murdered sleep!
Macbeth	Still it cries out!
Lady Macbeth	Who is it that thus cries?
Duncan	Macbeth hath murdered sleep!
Macbeth	I am afraid to think what I have done…
Lady Macbeth	Infirm of purpose!
	*Exit **Duncan**.*
Sisters	*[Chanting]* Now the charm Is wound up tight, Now the sky Begins to light…
Macbeth	This is a sorry sight.
Lady Macbeth	A foolish thought.
Macbeth	What are these hands?
Lady Macbeth	You do unbend your noble self.
Macbeth	The old man had so much blood –
Lady Macbeth	The sleeping and the dead are but as pictures.
Macbeth	To know my deed, 'twere best not know myself.

***Lady Macbeth** takes the dagger from **Macbeth**. **Macbeth** turns away and stands apart.*

Sisters	*[Chanting]* The air is chill,
	The sky is red,
	A raven croaks,
	A man is dead.
Lady Macbeth	A little water clears us of this deed.
Sisters	*[Chanting]* All hail!
	All hail!
	All hail!
Lady Macbeth	*[Placing a crown on **Macbeth**'s head]* All hail.
Macbeth	*[Facing the audience]* Blood will have blood.

Macbeth remains facing out over the audience and the Sisters return to their places by the stones for the next scene. Lady Macbeth also remains onstage.

Lady Macbeth	*[To the audience]* Duncan's dead,
	Others are accused and fled;
	My husband proclaimed king
	So my father's blood is paid.
	His spirit is at peace,
	But mine is not:
	Somewhere in this world my child lives,
	Unknown to me, and nameless,
	And until he's found I will not rest.
	Since I sent him with the nurse, I've had no word,
	But that's no mystery in troubled times like these;
	And even now, with peace restored, the kingdom ours,
	His life would not be safe.
	The Sisters' power that worked my husband to his deed
	Has made him mad, and he's grown murderous…
Macbeth	To be thus is nothing, but to be safely thus. We have scorch'd the snake, not killed it.
Lady Macbeth	His mind filled with howling phantoms –
Macbeth	Avaunt*! Quit my sight! Shake not thy gory locks at me!
Lady Macbeth	Bloody-faced spirits that haunt his soul –
Macbeth	The time has been that when the brains were out, the man would die.
Lady Macbeth	And make his crown a ring of burning fire That sears his skull.
Macbeth	Full of scorpions is my mind!
Lady Macbeth	He does not sleep, But lies awake and stares into the dark, And hears the whispering of secret tongues…
Girl	*[Whispering]* Beware!
Goodwife	*[Whispering]* Beware!
Crone	*[Whispering]* Beware!

86   *   *avaunt – go away*

Macbeth stares in their direction as they each raise a doll into the air.

Lady Macbeth   And sees strange visions filling him with horror…

Sisters   *[Whispering]* Beware Macduff. Beware the Thane of Fife.

Macbeth   Enough!

Lady Macbeth   And by these visions,
And by these voices,
He's urged on to further bloodshed.

Macbeth   The castle of Macduff I will surprise,
Seize upon Fife –
I am in blood steep'd so far –

Lady Macbeth   I could pity him
If I loved him,
And once I could have loved him.
Once there could have been a time –
But all that's finished with,
As some birth-strangled babe
Whose future's stifled in the crib.
His heart is fixed on blood, mine on my son,
So I'll send out in secret messengers
To find news of his whereabouts
And, when I hear it, keep that knowledge close
Until the time comes when my husband falls –
For fall he must:
A tyrant's only future is in dust –
And then my son shall rise, a blaze of light,
Star of the dawn,
A king true-born,
And so restore our people's stolen rights.

Lady Macbeth turns to go.

Macbeth   *[Turning to **Lady Macbeth**]* There shall be done a deed of
dreadful note.

*The **Macbeths** hold each other's gaze for a moment. Exit **Lady
Macbeth**. **Macbeth** remains onstage, and the **Sisters** by the
standing stones, for the next scene.*

Enter Grimm.

Grimm *[To the audience]* And who'll do that deed, eh? And more like it? Here's the chap, standing before you. I'm a man of many talents, me, and can turn my hand to most things – and that includes a bit o' throat-cutting.

Macbeth *[To Grimm]* Thou art the best o' th' cut-throats.

Grimm True, my lord. *[To the audience]* Though I say it myself, I ain't half bad at it. Not that it comes natural, mind. I wouldn't say that. No, takes a bit o' getting used to, it does. Especially the first time. But after that it gets easier alright.

Macbeth Is he dispatch'd?

Grimm My lord, his throat is cut.

Macbeth moves away.

[To the audience] Course, throat-cutting ain't my regular job here. That's be gatekeeper. The other's what you might call occasional employment; though the two do go well together, for with the one I let folks into the castle, and with the other I let them into the beyond – and there's many a one down there knocking at them gates that won't never be let out again. If you listen, you can hear them.

He kneels, puts his ear to the floor, and knocks.

There they go. Knock-knock, knock-knock, knock-knock –

Macbeth *[Snapping at Grimm]* Hold! Enough! Wake Duncan with thy knocking!

Grimm Sorry, my lord. *[Standing, to the audience]* Best do as he says. He's king, after all, and I'm his servant, and when a king commands, a servant obeys. That's the way of things in this world – and in the other, too, I reckon; for there are them as say that I ain't just servant to the king, but to the very devil himself, and that's what this Macbeth is – the Evil One incarnate. Well, so he may be, and if he is the king of hell, then I'm well set, for the devil's doorkeeper will have full employment for eternity.

Macbeth	How say'st thou? That Macduff denies his person At our great bidding?
Grimm	Macduff?
Macbeth	Macduff denies his person…
Grimm	Macduff is fled to England.
Macbeth	Fled to England?
Grimm	Aye, my lord.
Macbeth	Then comes my fit again!
Grimm	*[To the audience]* Followed close on its heels by a command for some new killing, I'll warrant. I know the signs by now.
Macbeth	Macduff is fled?
Grimm	Aye, my lord –
Macbeth	Give to th'edge o' th' sword his wife, his babes –
Grimm	His wife … his babes –
Macbeth	All unfortunate souls that trace him in his line!
Grimm	This deed … his wife –
Macbeth	His wife – his babes!
Grimm	This bloody deed…

Macbeth takes out a bag of coins and holds it out to Grimm.

Macbeth	No boasting like a fool.
Grimm	This deed I'll do.

Macbeth drops the bag into Grimm's hand. Exit Macbeth.

[Looking inside the bag] But not with my own hand. I don't have much stomach for killing women and kids. But I know them that has – villains who'll do anything for a coin and a crust, a lot less than I have here in this bag. It's a bad world where such folks live and walk, a wicked world, and the innocent are best off out of it. The way I sees it, I'm doing everybody a favour. Macbeth has his killing done, them as does it gets paid for their

pleasure, Macduff's missus and his kids gets sent to heaven, and I keep the gold and my hands and my conscience clean. So all are well content, and there ain't no crime in that.

*Exit **Grimm**. The **Wyrd Sisters** remain onstage for the next scene.*

Scene 21

· ·

Enter **Magg**.

Magg   *[Calling out and knocking]* Husband! Grimm! Are you there? Answer me! Don't you hear my knocking? *[Knocking loudly]* Husband! *[To the audience]* I see he's no better than he was: still can't do a job properly. He's supposed to be gatekeeper and let folks in, and here I am waiting to be let in, and here he is, not here. *[Knocking]* Open up, there! Open up, you mawkin★! Let me in before I batter the whole castle down about your ears! *[To the audience]* They says there's secrets hid in this place, that mournful ghosts and spirits walk and wail, and that the very stones themselves weep tears of blood. And if my husband don't get here soon I'll make a ghost of him, and he'll be weeping and wailing fit to drown out all the others. *[Knocking]* Grimm, you snail's fart! Open up!

Enter **Grimm**, *from the other side of the stage.*

Grimm   What's all this racket about? Who's knocking there?

Magg   Somebody who'll be knocking hard on your head if you don't get this gate open sharpish.

Grimm   Who dares threaten the king's gatekeeper?

Magg   You know who well enough.

Grimm   State your name and business.

Magg   My name's what it always was and my business is none of yours. Now open up!

Grimm   Not until I know who it is that asks and the nature of your business. Speak. I command you!

Magg   You command me?

Grimm   I do, and I shall be obeyed.

Magg   By who?

Grimm   By you!

★   *mawkin – a weakling*

Magg	Says who?
Grimm	Says me!
Magg	And since when have you the right to command anything of me?
Grimm	It's been common law all the way back to Adam that a man shall have the commanding of his wife –
Magg	Ha! So you do know who I am, then? Then you'll know as well that I'm the one to do the commanding, and I command you to let me in!
	She knocks loudly.
Grimm	Keep it down, Magg! It's early morning: you'll wake the whole castle!
Magg	I'll wake the dead if I must.
Grimm	Alright, stop knocking. I'll let you in.
	Grimm opens the gate.
Magg	That's better. Now. First of all, my business with you…
Grimm	Now, Magg – stop rolling up them sleeves, now – keep back – put them fists away – put them fists away! – I forbid you – don't come near me – stay where you are – heed your master's voice –
Magg	I'll heed no such thing for I have none!
Grimm	If you lay a hand on me it'll be the worse for you.
Magg	How d'you make that out?
Grimm	I have the king's favour, and he won't take kindly to it.
Magg	Have the king's favour, do you? Well, after I've spoke with her just now, I'll have the queen's favour, so then we'll be equal, and then I'll give you your beating.
Grimm	That's who your business is with, then? The queen?
Magg	It is.
Grimm	And what kind of business might it be? That's what I'm wondering.
Magg	I'm sure you are.

Grimm	Must be important.
Magg	It is.
Grimm	And secret, to bring you here so early.
Magg	That secret's for her ears alone.
Grimm	Let's hope the king don't find out about it, then.
Magg	There's no reason why he should.
Grimm	I'm the king's servant. I have my duty.
Magg	Grimm –
Grimm	Course, if I knew what the secret was, I'd be in a position to know whether the king should hear of it or not. Especially if there was some profit in it.
Magg	Why should there be profit in my business with the queen?
Grimm	Magg wouldn't be Magg if there wasn't some profit to be had. And Grimm wouldn't be Grimm if he didn't try to take his share of it.
Magg	Husband, you've learned a few tricks over the years and ain't half the fool you once was. So I'll tell you. My business is to do with the queen's child.
Grimm	The queen's child? I've never heard of any child!
Magg	Course you haven't, and neither has the king, nor anybody else. She kept it close, you see. It's the child she had by her first husband, that she put about had died. Only it didn't die. She had it sent away.
Grimm	Sent away?
Magg	On the very day her first husband was killed by her second, for fear he'd kill the child as well.
Grimm	How come you know all this?
Magg	She's been sending out to find it. A few trusted messengers. It's from one of them I have the whole story –
Grimm	Magg! I remember how you told me you found a child once, and it was on that very same day the queen sent hers away, and you sold it to some noblewoman…

Magg	That's right –
Grimm	And it seems to me that child you found must have been the queen's. Stands to reason, don't it?
Magg	It does –
Grimm	So all you've got to do is tell the queen the name of the woman you sold it to –
Magg	Which is the very thing I'm here to do. *[To the audience]* Sharp as a knife, this one.
Grimm	Magg, what a team we make! Why, this information could make us rich!
Magg	I had some such thought in my head myself.
Grimm	It's just like the old times come again – you and me, working together. Now, what was this woman's name?
Magg	What woman?
Grimm	The noblewoman.
Magg	And what noblewoman would that be?
Grimm	The one you sold the child to!
Magg	Now that would be telling.
Grimm	It would. So? What was it?
Magg	What was what?
Grimm	Her name!
Magg	Whose name?
Grimm	Don't come that with me, Magg! You know very well what I mean!
Magg	I do indeed, husband. And that's why I'm keeping that name to myself, cos the minute I tell you, you'll be off like a shot to tell the queen and keep the reward all to yourself.
Grimm	You think I'd do a thing like that?
Magg	I know you'd do a thing like that, which is why I'll tell the name only to the queen herself!

*Enter **Lady Macbeth**.*

Lady Macbeth	Then I'd better hear it.
Magg	My lady –
Lady Macbeth	But before I do, I must be sure that the child you found – and sold – was mine.
Magg	I'm certain it was, my lady.
Lady Macbeth	We'll soon know. In the message you sent to me, you said you found this child on the day my first husband was killed.
Magg	That's true. I remember it well.
Lady Macbeth	Where did you find it? What was the place?
Magg	The forest close by your first husband's castle.
Lady Macbeth	That's the way she would have gone. But it's a hard world, and there's more than one child been abandoned in it. Can you remember how the child was clothed?
Magg	I can, my lady.
Lady Macbeth	Tell me.
Magg	It was wrapped in a shawl of woven wool, red and green. And within the shawl, a blanket of fleece, to keep it from the cold.
Grimm	Don't she have a memory? Eh? Don't she, though, my lady?
Lady Macbeth	She does. She remembers well. It was my child she found.
Grimm	I never doubted it.
Lady Macbeth	Now tell me the name of the woman to whom you gave my child.
Magg	I will, my lady. It was the wife to Lord Macduff –
Grimm	Macduff? Did you say Macduff?
Magg	That's what I said.
Lady Macbeth	The man my husband fears most…
Grimm	*[To Magg]* Are you positive?
Magg	Course I am.
Lady Macbeth	He means some harm against him…
Grimm	*[To Magg]* You might be mistook.

Magg	I ain't mistook. I remember it perfectly.
Lady Macbeth	'The castle of Macduff I will surprise.' Those were his words –
Grimm	I think my wife has the wrong woman, my lady –
Magg	No, I don't!
Lady Macbeth	The wrong woman? What do you mean?
Magg	Yes, husband, what do you mean?
Grimm	I mean, her memory ain't what it was –
Lady Macbeth	You praised her memory but a little while since.
Magg	[Indignant] There ain't nothing wrong with my memory! Lady Macduff I said and Lady Macduff it was!
Grimm	No, it wasn't.
Magg	Yes, it was!
Grimm	You can't be sure!
Magg	I can and I am!
Lady Macbeth	[To Grimm] You are fearful. Why are you so afraid it should be Macduff's wife who has my child?
Grimm	Fearful? Me? I ain't fearful, my lady –
Lady Macbeth	Your face says otherwise. There's something known to you.
Grimm	No –
Magg	He's keeping something back, alright.
Lady Macbeth	'There shall be done a deed of dreadful note.' His words again. [To Grimm] Tell me what you know!
Grimm	I don't know nothing!
Magg	Leave him to me, my lady. I'll have the truth out of him –
Grimm	There ain't no truth to tell, and even if there was, it's best you don't know it!
Lady Macbeth	Whatever this truth is, or is not, you will speak it to me now.
Magg	You've rumbled yourself, Grimm. Out with it.
Grimm	Alright, I'll tell. Men are to be sent to Macduff's castle.

Lady Macbeth	Men?
Grimm	Armed men.
Lady Macbeth	But Macduff has fled to England. What were their orders?
Grimm	I'm only the gatekeeper –
Lady Macbeth	You know! Tell me! What orders were they given? Who were they told to kill?
	A pause.
Grimm	His wife, his babes, all –
Lady Macbeth	Oh, God! What monster's this I've made? Sisters, we did our work too well. Blood will have blood. But not this time, no! This time I'll pluck the dagger from his hands. *[To **Grimm**]* They've not yet gone?
Grimm	No, my lady, but they're making ready –
Lady Macbeth	I'll send a messenger, choose the swiftest horse. She must be warned, flee with her children – with my child – to England and her husband. I'll go there myself – help Macduff against my husband – his time's done – lay the path clear for my son – yes – all shall be well –
	Lady Macbeth prepares to leave.
Magg	My lady –
Lady Macbeth	Why do you keep me?
Magg	There was to be reward –
Lady Macbeth	You want payment.
Magg	I brought you information –
Grimm	I saved your child's life –
Lady Macbeth	Of course you want payment. You must be rewarded. Here. Take this bracelet. And my rings, all of them. This necklace too. That will fetch a good price. More? My crown. It's pure gold. It will sell in the marketplace. Wrap them all in my cloak, it's lined with ermine. I give you all, everything – which to me is nothing to the life of my child.

*Lady Macbeth goes to one side of the stage and takes up a position facing out over the audience. **Magg** starts to place the jewellery and crown in the cloak.*

Magg	This is better than I looked for.
Grimm	Not a bad haul. Bundle it up quick and let's be gone.
Magg	Why the rush?
Grimm	When she finds out the truth –
Magg	I thought you told her –
Grimm	In part. Them sent to kill Macduff's family have already left. I should know. I sent them there myself.
Magg	You?
Grimm	On the king's orders. And when she finds out her child's dead, and I had a hand in it –
Magg	You're right. We'd best make tracks. *[Throwing the bundle to Grimm]* Here you are, husband. Just like old times. Back on the road.
Grimm	Living on our wits.
Magg	Those of us as 'ave 'em.
Grimm	Where shall we make for?
Magg	Who knows? Who cares? Looks like there's going to be war again. War and strife, that's the tune we march to. War and strife and troubled times. For where there's trouble, there's a living to be made.

Exit Magg and Grimm.

Lady Macbeth	*[To the audience]* The Thane of Fife, he had a wife... She's killed – the whole household put to death – her children slaughtered – my child – the oldest boy... I saw him once. I didn't know. And now he's dead. My child is dead.

The Thane of Fife, he had a wife;
That wife, she had a child...

No more no more no more no more no more...

He'll not long outlive them. Does he believe he cannot die? The Sisters have deceived him, as they deceive us all. Listen! The dogs are howling, the pack's running: they smell his blood. Macduff will come for vengeance, and when vengeance strikes, it strikes all…

My child's dead – bones in the ground… I should mourn. I should weep. I should tear my hair… But I have no tears. My eyes are stones, and stone my heart: it does not beat, I cannot weep. But listen! There's weeping… Who is it? Who weeps? A lost soul. Where? That way, follow it – take the path – but quiet, soft – don't cry, don't weep… There… It's all right… Hush… Hush…

She moves to the centre of the standing stones.

Girl	Hush!
Goodwife	Someone's coming…
Crone	Footsteps approaching…
Girl	Following the path…
Goodwife	The track of their tale…
Crone	Unwinding here, where all stories end.
Lady Macbeth	Once upon a time there was a girl and she had a daddy and they were very happy but the girl wanted a husband and a baby of her own –

No
That's an old tale.
It's done with now –
The mouth silent, the tongue still,
No story left to tell.
Nothing remains but these
Old stones, cold, hard,
Dead.
Do they speak? Do the dead stones speak?
Listen –
No sound, no one speaks, there's no one there –
But there's that weeping;

I can hear it again – somebody weeping –
Who is it, who's weeping?
Father? Is it you?
My child? Are you here?
My husband?
Your blood's not on my hands –
Yet … here's a spot –
And another, and another –
Whose blood is this?
Whose blood?
Why do my hands weep?
My nails, fingers, weeping blood –
Wash it off, wash off the blood
Here in this pool –
A little water clears us of this deed –
Oh! Who's this? Whose face?
See her – there she is –
Down there in the black water –
Fallen so far, dived so deep –
Her poor body's broken
And she has bad dreams…
Is that why she weeps?
I'll touch her face,
A girl's face,
A bride's face,
A mother's face,
A widow's face.
Cold, cold,
Her face,
My face –
A dead face,
A dead face…

Exit **Lady Macbeth**. *The* **Wyrd Sisters** *remain onstage for the next scene.*

Scene 22

Girl   She's gone.

Goodwife   Her tale's done.

Crone   No one remembers it…

Girl   Not even the earth.

Goodwife   Her name's lost.

Crone   The earth has forgotten her…

Girl   And us, the earth is forgetting us.

Goodwife   Her tale is our tale…

Crone   And that's done too.

Girl   We are stones once more.

Goodwife   We are stones only…

Crone	And the wind that scratches them…
Girl	And the rain that weeps over them…
Goodwife	Old stones crumbling…
Crone	Broken teeth on the hillside.
	In turn, each Sister rises and picks up one of the dolls.
Girl	The Girl…
Goodwife	The Goodwife…
Crone	The Crone…
Sisters	No more.
	Exit Sisters.

THE END

Activities

Year 8

KEY STAGE 3 FRAMEWORK OBJECTIVES	RELEVANT ACTIVITIES CHAPTER(S)
Sentence Level	
12 Degrees of formality	A Persuasive Letter
Word Level	
8 Use linguistic terms	Poetic Forms
11 Figurative vocabulary	Poetic Forms
12 Formality and word choice	Poetic Forms
Reading	
3 Notemaking formats	Themes; The 'fiend-like queen'
4 Versatile reading	Themes; The 'fiend-like queen'
5 Trace developments	The Structure of *Lady Macbeth*; Themes; The 'fiend-like queen'
7 Implied and explicit meanings	Themes
10 Development of key ideas	The Structure of *Lady Macbeth*; Themes; Poetic Forms
Writing	
1 Effective planning	Writing a New Scene; Writing a Newspaper Report
2 Anticipate reader/audience reaction	Writing a New Scene; Writing a Newspaper Report
3 Writing to reflect	The 'fiend-like queen'; Writing a Newspaper Report
7 Establish the tone	Poetic Forms; Writing a New Scene
10 Effective information	Writing a Newspaper Report
12 Formal description	Writing a Newspaper Report
13 Present a case persuasively	The 'fiend-like queen'; A Persuasive Letter
14 Develop an argument	The 'fiend-like queen'; A Persuasive Letter
16 Balanced analysis	Writing a Newspaper Report
17 Integrate evidence	Writing a Newspaper Report
Speaking and Listening	
1 Evaluate own speaking	The 'fiend-like queen'
3 Formal presentation	The 'fiend-like queen'
5 Questions to clarify or refine	The 'fiend-like queen'
6 Evaluate own listening	The 'fiend-like queen'
7 Listen for a specific purpose	The 'fiend-like queen'
9 Evaluate own contributions	The 'fiend-like queen'
10 Hypothesis and speculation	The 'fiend-like queen'
11 Building on others	The 'fiend-like queen'; Writing a New Scene
12 Varied roles in discussion	The 'fiend-like queen'
13 Evaluate own drama skills	Writing a New Scene
14 Dramatic techniques	Writing a New Scene
15 Work in role	Writing a New Scene
16 Collaborative presentation	Writing a New Scene

Year 9

KEY STAGE 3 FRAMEWORK OBJECTIVES	RELEVANT ACTIVITIES CHAPTER(S)
Sentence Level	
3 Degrees of formality	A Persuasive Letter
Reading	
1 Information retrieval	Themes
3 Notemaking at speed	Themes; The 'fiend-like queen'
7 Compare texts	The Structure of *Lady Macbeth*; Themes
14 Analyse scenes	Poetic Forms
Writing	
3 Formal essay	Writing a Newspaper Report
7 'infotainment'	Writing a Newspaper Report
8 Poetic form and meaning	Poetic Forms
9 Integrate information	Writing a Newspaper Report
11 Descriptive detail	Writing a Newspaper Report
13 Influence audience	The 'fiend-like queen'; A Persuasive Letter
14 Counter-argument	The 'fiend-like queen'; A Persuasive Letter
16 Balanced analysis	Writing a Newspaper Report
17 Cite textual evidence	The 'fiend-like queen'
Speaking and Listening	
1 Evaluate own talk	The 'fiend-like queen'
2 Standard English	The 'fiend-like queen'
3 Interview techniques	Writing a New Scene
4 Evaluate own listening skills	The 'fiend-like queen'
5 Compare points of view	The 'fiend-like queen'
7 Identify underlying issues	The 'fiend-like queen'
8 Evaluate own contributions	The 'fiend-like queen'
9 Considered viewpoint	The 'fiend-like queen'
10 Group organization	The 'fiend-like queen'
11 Evaluate own drama skills	Writing a New Scene
12 Drama techniques	Writing a New Scene
14 Convey character and atmosphere	Writing a New Scene
15 Critical evaluation	Writing a New Scene

The Structure of Lady Macbeth

Lady Macbeth follows the turbulent life of a woman called Gruach from girlhood to her death. The second part of the play covers the same story as Shakespeare's play, *Macbeth*.

The structure of the plot in *Lady Macbeth* is complex, as it covers many decades, and power shifts between the characters.

1   Remind yourself of the sequence of events by putting the following scenes into their correct order. (These scenes appear only in the play, *Lady Macbeth*.)

Gruach sees Beoedhe die in a dream and plans vengeance.

Gruach, daughter of Beoedhe, consults the Wyrd Sisters about her future husband.

Duncan and Macbeth kill King Malcolm and MacRory Gillacomgain.

MacRory Gillacomgain and Finnleach fight. Finnleach is killed.

Gruach gives her baby son to the
Nurse and urges them to escape.

Gruach helps Thorfinn escape from
MacRory Gillacomgain.

The Nurse is killed and the baby is
found by Magg, who sells him to Lady
Macduff.

Macbeth (formerly known as
Thorfinn) returns to re-claim his land.
He forms an alliance with Duncan.

Gruach marries Macbeth.

King Malcolm banishes Beoedhe
and gives Gruach to MacRory
Gillacomgain as a wife.

2   The following events occur in both *Lady Macbeth* and in Shakespeare's *Macbeth*. Sort them into the correct order.

Macbeth orders the killing of Macduff's family.

Magg tells Lady Macbeth that she found her baby and sold him to Lady Macduff.

Macbeth and Lady Macbeth kill King Duncan. Macbeth becomes king.

Macbeth is warned by the Wyrd Sisters to beware Macduff.

Lady Macbeth becomes mentally unstable, tortured by grief and horror, then dies.

In Shakespeare's *Macbeth*, the story is taken one step further: after Lady Macbeth's death, Macbeth is slain by Macduff. Duncan's son, Malcolm, prepares to become King of Scotland.

Themes

● ●

There are many themes that weave through the playscript *Lady Macbeth*. (Many are also present in Shakespeare's *Macbeth*.)

1   Compile a list of all the themes that you can identify. Your list might start like this:

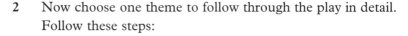

- blood
- death
- loyalty and friendship
- weapons and violence...

2   Now choose one theme to follow through the play in detail. Follow these steps:

Step 1

Skim the playscript to find some examples of where the theme emerges.

Step 2

Note down the examples, including a quotation and a brief explanation of context (where it is in the play) for each one.

Step 3

Decide how the theme is used each time and the effect it has on the audience.

You may wish to record your notes in a grid like the one below. This example focuses on the theme of blood.

Quotation	Context	Effect
'From the dark of the blood that runs in her veins...' (page 16)	A Wyrd Sister explains how Gruach called them up.	Sounds mysterious, as if Gruach has supernatural powers that she isn't aware of.
'...the face that she sees will be bloody...' (page 17)	A Wyrd Sister describes the face of Gruach's future husband.	Hints that the man will be either a victim, or inflict violence on others. This makes the reader curious.
'The earth needs blood...' (page 19)	Setting the scene for the fight between Finnleach and MacRory.	Makes the world seem a cruel place that needs people's blood like a plant needs water.

3   If you have a copy of Shakespeare's *Macbeth*, skim the text to try to find a reference to your chosen theme. When you find one, repeat Steps 2 and 3 on page 109.

As before, the example below focuses on the theme of blood.

Macbeth: Will all great Neptune's ocean wash this blood
Clean from my hand? No: this my hand will rather
The multitudinous seas incarnadine,
Making the green one red.

Macbeth, II.ii.63–66

This quotation is from Act 2 Scene 2. It is spoken by Macbeth as he looks at his blood-stained hands after murdering King Duncan.

The image suggests that nothing will take the blood (and guilt) off Macbeth's hands - instead of washing them clean in the sea, the blood would turn the whole sea red.

If you have difficulty in finding your own examples in Shakespeare's *Macbeth*, here are some quotations that you might find helpful:

Death – Act 2, Scene 3, line 49 'The night has been unruly...'

Friendship/loyalty – Act 1, Scene 7, line 12 'He's here in double trust...'

Power – Act 5, Scene 2, line 20 'Now does he feel his title...'

Weapons/violence – Act 2, Scene 1, line 33 'Is this a dagger...'

The 'fiend-like queen'

At the end of Shakespeare's play, Macbeth and Lady Macbeth are referred to as 'this dead butcher and his fiend-like queen' (V.ix.36).

1   Hold a debate to decide whether this description of Lady Macbeth is justified. (Refer only to this playscript, *Lady Macbeth*.)

Step 1

Split into two groups: one group to gather evidence for Lady Macbeth, the other to gather evidence against Lady Macbeth.

Step 2

Within your group, discuss Lady Macbeth, referring only to this playscript. Make sure that everyone has a turn to speak and that their views are taken into consideration. Identify actions and speeches in the playscript that can be used as evidence to support your views.

Step 3

In your group, choose one person to take notes. As a group, decide on the strongest arguments to support your case. Your notes may start like this:

Lady Macbeth IS NOT 'fiend-like'	Lady Macbeth IS 'fiend-like'
● She is only trying to regain land that her ancestors owned – 'My people held this land long before yours' (Scene 5)	● She meddles with magic and the supernatural and Duncan describes the Picts as 'Witches and devil-worshippers! Enemies of all that's holy!' (Scene 7)
● She takes pity on Thorfinn (Scene 4)	● She is cold – she refuses to be intimate with her husband

- She is brave and outspoken when captured – '…I see no justice here. Only cruel vengeance, tyranny and persecution!' (Scene 7)

- She is right to seek revenge for the death of her father

- …

- She lets resentment fester and is unforgiving – 'I pray that…/…my spirit's ills become a nest/Of writhing vipers, spitting poison, and/Infecting all' (Scene 8)

- She is ambitious and calculating

- …

Step 4

As a group, decide on:

- how you are going to present your case effectively
- a speaker to put forward the group's views.

Step 5

The debate begins. In turn, each speaker must present their group's case to the whole class.

Step 6

Other members of the class should now be invited to contribute to the debate. This is your chance to make any points you feel will help your group to win the debate.

Step 7

Hold a vote to reach a judgement on whether or not Lady Macbeth is 'fiend-like'.

2   After the debate, discuss – as a whole class – which group's presentation was most effective. For each presentation, decide on:

- what its strengths were
- how it could have been developed further.

3   Finally, think about your own contribution to the group discussion above. Did you put forward your views strongly enough? Did you listen carefully to other people's ideas? Make a note of how you could improve your contribution to group discussions in the future.

A Persuasive Letter

Re-read Scene 18 (pages 80–85), thinking about the influence that Lady Macbeth has over her husband. She is a strong character, who knows her husband's strengths and weaknesses. She succeeds in persuading him to commit murder even though this is against his instincts and better judgement.

In Shakespeare's *Macbeth*, Lady Macbeth receives a letter from her husband explaining that the Wyrd Sisters (or Witches, as they are called in Shakespeare's play) have predicted that one day he will be king. Imagine you are Lady Macbeth and write a reply to send to your husband before he arrives home.

In the letter, persuade him to:

● take note of what the Sisters have said
● take action to make what they have said come true
● convince King Duncan to visit their home
● plan Duncan's murder.

Also:

● give reasons for what you are suggesting – choose ones that you know will appeal to Macbeth

● use rhetorical devices, to give your viewpoint impact

● try to anticipate Macbeth's objections and give some counter-arguments.

Rhetorical devices

Remember: these rhetorical devices can help to persuade a reader or audience.

Rhetorical questions: questions which do not require an answer but address the audience directly and draw attention to an issue

Repetition: repeating an idea or image helps to reinforce it in the audience's mind

Exaggeration: this can make an idea more dramatic and urgent

Emotive language: this will stir up the audience's emotions, triggering powerful feelings such as pity, anger, envy, greed, etc.

Flattery: this makes the audience feel good about themselves and makes them more sympathetic to your views

Short sentences: including some short sentences can have great impact

---

Step 1

Decide:

- how formal your letter will be
- how explicit you are going to be about your hopes and ambitions.

Step 2

Decide how you are going to open your letter. You could start your letter with one of the following openings:

My darling, hero, husband...

Macbeth,
Great things lie ahead...

Dear Macbeth,
Your letter filled me with excitement...

To my most noble lord and
husband...

Step 3

Write your letter. Remember to use some rhetorical devices.

Step 4

Read through your letter. Is there anything you could improve? Ask a partner for his or her opinion.

Step 5

Make any final changes to your letter.

Poetic Forms

1   Read the following extracts from *Lady Macbeth*.

Sisters:

We weave the webs
That bind men fast,
From breath to death
From first to last.
From joy to pain,
From grave to birth,
We set men walking
On the earth
And shape their fates
With tales and songs,
And tell their lives
With crooked tongues.

Magg:

My husband's a fool! As if I never knew it. Of course, I knew it. I always
knew it. Why else did I marry him? If a woman's wise, she'll marry a fool,
and the wiser the woman, the greater the fool she'll marry. Which must
make me wiser than Solomon, for there's no greater fool in the Christian
nor the Pagan world than my husband. The only wise thing he ever did was
marry me, and that was because his mother threw him out on account she
couldn't put up with his foolishness no more.

Macbeth:

Once more my feet tread on this native earth
Where I was born, and which I've come to claim
With flame and sword. My men are armed
And ripe for war, which soon shall be unleashed
To rock this juggling world; then vengeance howl
Throughout the stormy skies, until that man
Who killed my father falls beneath my blade:
So falls his spirit down to deepest hell.
Come, Furies! Shake your venomed serpent locks,
And gaze with bloody looks upon my cause!
For I'll not rest until this deed is done,
Nor sheathe my rage until the battle's won!

a) How does the layout of each speech differ? (Think about line length, and whether it is poetry or prose.)

b) Which speech uses rhyme? Give an example.

c) Which speech has a regular rhythm to each line? Give an example.

2 In most of his plays, Shakespeare matches certain forms of speech with certain types of character.

Using your knowledge of the above extracts, try to match the forms described below to the correct type of character.

Forms	Type of character
1 Short, simple, rhyming verse	A Noble, powerful, prominent
2 Prose, with no rhythm or pattern (like everyday speech)	B Simple, minor, uneducated
3 Rhythmic, poetic language, rich in imagery	C Magical, supernatural or comic

3 Why do you think the author of this playscript, David Calcutt, and Shakespeare choose different forms for different characters? (Think about variety and ease of identifying characters.)

BLANK VERSE

Read through Macbeth's speech from *Lady Macbeth* on page 116 carefully once more.

It is written in a style called blank verse, which uses a poetic rhythm called iambic pentameter. This means:

● each line has ten beats (syllables)
● the beats are divided into pairs (iambic feet)
● each iambic foot contains one stressed and one unstressed syllable.

(Note: this is the overall pattern of the text, but not all lines fit this pattern exactly.)

In the grid below, two lines from the speech are divided out into syllables and marked to show the stressed (/) and unstressed (U) syllables.

1st iambic foot		2nd iambic foot		3rd iambic foot		4th iambic foot		5th iambic foot	
1	2	3	4	5	6	7	8	9	10
U	/	U	/	U	/	U	/	U	/
To	rock	this	jugg	ling	world	then	veng	eance	howl
U	/	U	/	U	/	U	/	U	/
Through	out	the	storm	y	skies	un	til	that	man

1 Use a similar grid to divide out the final two lines of the same speech into stressed and unstressed syllables:

For I'll not rest until this deed is done,

Nor sheathe my rage until the battle's won!

2 Now try writing two lines of your own in the same poetic form – two lines of blank verse in iambic pentameter.

You could continue Macbeth's speech for two lines, perhaps, or write the lines for another character of your choice.

Writing a New Scene

At the end of Scene 11, Duncan and Macbeth go into a tent to plot their course of action. In *Lady Macbeth*, the audience does not witness this scene: not knowing exactly what the men have planned adds to the suspense. Instead, we just witness the effects of their plotting – the murders of Malcolm and MacRory (pages 64–67).

With a partner, write a short script for the scene inside the tent. Follow the steps below.

Step 1

Together, brainstorm the content, and then the mood, of the scene. Use a spider diagram like the one below to record your ideas. You might want to jot down:

- reasons for murder
- emotions to be conveyed
- the pact agreed between the two men
- the plans to actually kill
- the relationship between the two men
- secrecy and danger
- how the meeting ends (e.g. perhaps with an interruption).

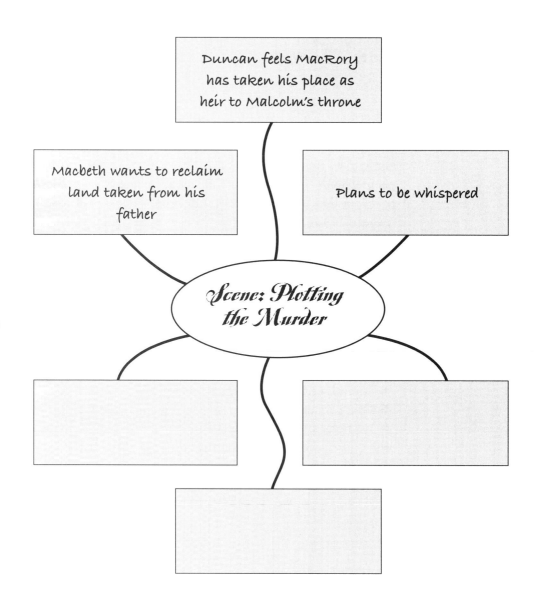

Duncan feels MacRory has taken his place as heir to Malcolm's throne

Macbeth wants to reclaim land taken from his father

Plans to be whispered

Scene: Plotting the Murder

Step 2

Before you start writing, remind yourself of the following conventions:

● Use stage directions to indicate where the scene is set
● Write the characters' names before their lines

- Write the characters' lines as direct speech
- Use stage directions to indicate tone or actions, or the use of props.

(It might help you to look back over *Lady Macbeth* and see these conventions put into practice.)

Step 3

Write your first draft, trying out different ideas and words. Keep re-reading what you have written as you write it – this will help you to check you are conveying the mood and content you planned in Step 1.

Step 4

When you are happy with your script, practise performing it with your partner. Remember to think about:

- how you will create a mood of conspiracy
- your tone of voice
- your gestures and body language
- where to include dramatic pauses
- how you can emphasize certain words for effect.

Step 5

Perform your scene in front of another pair, or the class. Invite comments on the content and presentation.

Step 6

Invite your audience to interview you in role, asking questions about your motives, your feelings and your relationship with your co-conspirator. Give your answers in role, too, thinking carefully about your character's personality, background and ambitions.

Step 7

After the interview, evaluate your performance:

What were your strengths?

What aspects do you feel you could improve upon?

Writing a Newspaper Report

You are a newspaper journalist and you have been asked to report on the murder of King Duncan at Macbeth's castle. You have been to the castle, seen the corpse and interviewed some of the people in residence at the time of the killing.

Here are your notes:

- King Duncan stabbed to death during the night
- His sons have fled – are they guilty?
- Bloodied daggers have been found next to the guards
- Macbeth says he killed the guards on discovering the king's body and assuming they had murdered the king
- Lady Macbeth appears unwell – fainted on hearing the news
- Peasant woman, Magg, claims she saw a ghost who told her who the murderer is
- Macbeth due to be crowned king
- General atmosphere of suspicion and fear

You have 30 minutes to write your article, before it goes to press. Make sure you include:

- a headline
- a by-line
- an introduction that states who, what, where, when and how
- quotations from witnesses
- facts and opinions
- descriptive detail
- some sort of conclusion.

Remember to:

- allow time to re-read your work, keeping your target audience in mind
- proof-read your article, to correct any spelling and punctuation errors.

Further Activities

1   Do some research about the time in which *Lady Macbeth* is set. Use a variety of sources to find out about:

- the Picts
- the Norsemen
- castles in Scotland and Northumbria
- King Macbeth, who ruled from 1040 to 1057.

2   Recount the story of *Lady Macbeth*, in your own words, to a partner. Change the mood, tone and speed of your re-telling to reflect different parts of the story and to maintain your listener's interest.

3   Think about the roles of Magg and Grimm. What do they add to **Lady Macbeth**? Think about:

- how they echo the main plot in their search for power and wealth
- the husband and wife relationship (you could compare this with that of the Macbeths)
- the vices they display
- how they influence the main plot (e.g. finding Lady Macbeth's baby).

4   Choose a short scene from the play and re-write it in prose. Use either the first person narrative (I...) or the third person narrative (He...).

Remember: your audience will have nothing to see, so you need to describe the action in detail.

LADY MACBETH ACTIVITIES

LADY MACBETH ACTIVITIES

LADY MACBETH ACTIVITIES

OXFORD Playscripts

An exciting series that adapts modern novels and classic texts – perfect for using in the classroom and for performing.

Oxford Modern Playscripts

Across the Barricades; Joan Lingard, adapted by David Ian Neville; 0198320795

Brother in the Land; Robert Swindells, adapted by Joe Standerline; 0198320841

Johnny and the Dead; Terry Pratchett, adapted by Stephen Briggs; 0198314922

The Amazing Maurice and his Educated Rodents; Terry Pratchett, adapted by Stephen Briggs; 0198314949

The Snake-stone; adapted from her own novel by Berlie Doherty; 0198320876

The Turbulent Term of Tyke Tiler; adapted from her own novel by Gene Kemp; 019831499X

The Demon Headmaster; Gillian Cross, adapted by Adrian Flynn; 0198320647

Oxford Classic Playscripts

The Canterbury Tales; Geoffrey Chaucer, adapted by Martin Riley; 0198320639

Dracula; Bram Stoker, adapted by David Calcutt; 0198318987

Dr Faustus; Christopher Marlowe, adapted by Geraldine McCaughrean; 0198320868

Frankenstein; Mary Shelley, adapted by Philip Pullman; 0198314981

Lady Macbeth; David Calcutt; 0198320833

The Valley of Fear; Arthur Conan Doyle, adapted by Adrian Flynn; 019832085X

For more information or to request your inspection copy of any of the Playscripts titles, please call customer services on +44 (0) 1536 741068

www.OxfordSecondary.co.uk